Sophie

A ROYAL WEDDING SOUVENIR 1999

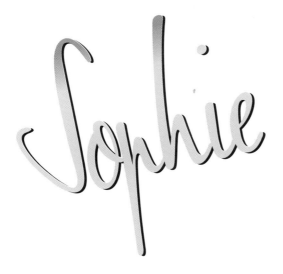

Sophie

A ROYAL WEDDING SOUVENIR 1999

NOAM FRIEDLANDER

CHAMELEON

First published in Great Britain in 1999 by Chameleon Books

an imprint of **André Deutsch Ltd**

76 Dean Street

London W1V 5HA

André Deutsch Ltd is a subsidiary of **VCI plc**

www.vci.co.uk

Design: **Neal Townsend** for **Essential**

Picture research: **Kay Rowley** for **Essential**

The right of Noam Friedlander to be identified as the author of this work has been
asserted by her in accordance with the Copyright, Designs and Patents Act 1988.

1 3 5 7 9 10 8 6 4 2

Reprographics by Jade Reprographics

Printed in Great Britain by Jarrold Book Printing Ltd

A catalogue record for this book is available from the British Library.

ISBN 0-233-99710-5

For Evelyn.

Acknowledgements

Thanks to everyone at Essential Books and to Jane Phillimore.

Sources

Hello! magazine, OK! magazine, People magazine, Majesty magazine, the
Express and the Sunday Express, the Daily Mail, the Mail on Sunday and
You magazine, The Times, The Sunday Times, the Telegraph and the
Sunday Telegraph, the Sun, the News of the World, the Mirror and the
Sunday Mirror, the London Evening Standard, the Scotsman, the Herald,
the BBC, ITN and The Macmillan Nurses Cancer Relief Fund.

Contents

Dreaming of Princes & Ponies

Ickford is the kind of quiet, pretty, staunchly middle-class village, situated in the lush green Buckinghamshire countryside, where small girls dream of ponies, princes and being loved by everybody. Few, of course, ever manage to accomplish all three of these, which is why, when Christopher and Mary Rhys-Jones gave birth to their second child and first daughter, Sophie Helen, they could have no idea that she was going to marry a prince when she grew up. The ponies they always hoped to be able to give her, the love they were sure of – but a prince? Despite there being some blue blood in the family (Christopher's family was distantly related to both the Queen and the late Diana, Princess of Wales), the Rhys-Jones had no idea that they would ever be on intimate terms with such esteemed in-laws.

In the distant past Christopher's family had, in fact, warred with Royal families, when in the eleventh century Elystan Glodrydd, Prince of Ferrig and his son, Cadwagan bloodily defended their land from the invading English. Sophie's maternal family could boast almost as long a lineage, the former Mary O'Sullivan having familial roots in Bantry Bay, County Cork, if not one quite as colourful.

The All Saints church in Brenchley village, attended by the Rhys-Jones family.

A view of the charming village where Sophie grew up.

Sophie was born on 20 January 1965, in the university city of Oxford at the Nuffield Maternity Home, from where she was taken to her parents' home in Ickford, to meet her elder brother David. With an expanded family, the small thatched cottage did not meet their needs for long. In 1968 the family moved to a larger Georgian home in the picturesque Kent hamlet of Brenchley, near Royal Tunbridge Wells.

Brenchley, which has won numerous best-kept village awards, is situated in the heart of the Kentish Weald. Like Ickford it is staunchly middle-class, prettier but no less private. It is small, with a tiny village green flanked by the old post office, the Bull public house (which, much later in her life Sophie and her friends would frequent noisily and happily) and dominated by the imposing All Saints church.

By all accounts Sophie had a happy childhood in this warm, close-knit community. She never strayed far out of the area until her move to London some years later. All her schools and friends were to be found within a ten-mile radius of her Brenchley base. This meant that even as a young girl she could walk, cycle or ride to visit friends, playgrounds and playing fields. It was a carefree time, for Brenchley was, and some say still is, exactly the kind of place where people can go about their business unmolested and untroubled. Locals won't say too much about the Rhys-Joneses, as they understand how much they value their privacy. It's that kind of place. The most that one local resident would comment is: 'They are a very warm and loving family.'

Sophie herself has commented positively on the protective stability of her home life, realizing that having such a childhood, 'Sets you up for anything you take on in life.' She also acknowledged that it gave her 'confidence' and 'security'. Her parents, now retired, still live in Homestead Farmhouse, the same seventeenth-century home in which Sophie grew up, and enjoy the benefits of the Brenchley lifestyle.

Elsewhere in the south of England, just ten months before Sophie's birthday, her fiancé was born in quite different circumstances. Edward was the last Royal birth in Buckingham Palace. Compared to Sophie's childhood, his well-documented life was nowhere near as relaxed. As a Royal, his destiny was to be forever in the public eye, with his every move scrutinized. However, as the youngest of four children, with Charles already fifteen years old and his sister, Anne also a teenager, Edward was lucky enough to have older siblings who would look out for him, and advise him on Royal behaviour.

Prince Andrew, then aged four, was close enough in age to be considered the same generation as Edward – he was also nearly the same age as Sophie's brother, David. It's understandable that Andrew and Edward developed a close bond from an early age.

Edward also undoubtedly benefited from the fact that his mother was able to spend more time with him, as she cut back on some of her Royal duties. Of course, HM The Queen and Prince Philip were also more experienced parents by then, and allowed Edward to develop at his own pace, unencumbered as Charles and Anne had been with many Royal duties. Yet Edward's world, filled as it was with Royal protocol, rules and tradition, was still far removed from Sophie's rather more straightforward middle-class existence.

As the young Sophie was growing up, her father, Christopher initially worked for the London Chemical Company, before becoming an overseas representative for a firm of car manufacturers and, prior to his retirement, importing and exporting tyres to Hungary. Her mother, meanwhile, was PA to an estate agent.

Sophie's parents were not especially wealthy and they had to work hard to provide Sophie and David with a private education. Her mother, Mary, whose father had been a bank manager and who had learned the benefits of hard work first-hand, took in typing to earn extra money for the family. She advertised her typing skills in her local parish magazine *Roundabout*, charging £4.50 an hour to type 'reports, letters, theses, CVs and book manuscripts'. Mary would type such documents in their brightly painted yellow kitchen, surrounded by cooking utensils and a multi-coloured kitchen unit. Not much changed over the years. The same kitchen unit was commented on by many of the journalists who visited the house after Sophie had started dating the Prince.

Sophie's first school was Nash House, the junior school of Dulwich College Preparatory School in Cranbrook, Kent. Taking on pupils from age three to thirteen (they move on to the prep school after they turn six), it is situated about two miles away from the much larger Cranbrook School, which is in the centre of the town. Because there are no bustling shops or busy roads to distract pupils, Dulwich has a serene atmosphere. Not for Dulwich pupils the constant sound of cars, buses and shoppers. Instead, there are rolling hills and a graveyard beyond the school walls.

Whilst at Nash House, Sophie was popular with the teachers, although most definitely not a prissy goody-goody, and she had a solid group of playmates. She spent her free time playing with her friends, running around the sports fields or playing games at one another's houses. One of her next-door neighbours in Brenchley remembered that 'Sophie was a lovely little girl, a real chatterbox. Our door was always open and she and sometimes

HM The Queen and Sophie Rhys-Jones horseriding together at Windsor.

Sophie's parents, Christopher and Mary Rhys-Jones.

her brother, David used to come round to play here.' Sophie, like all other little girls of that age who lived in the country, loved horses but was one of the few in her close group of friends who didn't actually own one. This didn't deter her, of course, from joining in all the fun along with the rest of her gang.

Sophie also had another childhood love – cooking – a passion she shares with Prince Edward (the two of them often experiment with new recipes in the kitchen). At school she would make peppermint creams for the village fair and proved herself to be a good cook (she won second prize for her efforts). Tellingly, her choice of recipe gives away one of her darkest secrets: Sophie has always had a sweet tooth and she is a self-confessed chocoholic. She can't eat just one: 'I have to have the lot,' she has revealed.

Sophie has painted a picture of her early school life as idyllic, and it's hard to find any argument with that statement. She was attentive, eager to learn and popular. But, of course, Nash House was as much about learning to co-exist with fellow pupils and respond positively to teachers and authority, the more intensive business of learning subjects by rote was still to come. At the age of six Sophie moved up to the prep school situated on the same site, Dulwich Preparatory School.

Dance, Ballerina, Dance

At Dulwich Prep, Sophie discovered another of the pleasures so loved by small girls when she took ballet and dancing lessons with the wife of the director of Sadler's Wells, Pearl Westlake. In those far-off days before under-elevens had discovered pop music, fashion and boys, donning a tutu and twirling in front of a full-length mirror with other like-minded girls was the height of fulfilment. Ballet classes at the age of six for bubbly, friendly Sophie meant a chance to show off and impress her peers. It also offered her a good opportunity to form firm friendships, which she surely did when she was partnered at class with fellow Brenchley resident, Sarah Sienisi. Theirs has proved itself to be a lifelong friendship, with the two of them making important decisions and moves together as they grew up.

Dulwich Prep provided much more than a firm basis on which Sophie could build her academic career. She further honed her social skills, impressing both teachers and pupils, making friends, and proving popular with boys and girls alike. It is telling, however, that ballet classes are the best-remembered tutorials of her early school life.

Scenes from Sophie's happy schooldays.

At the age of eleven Sophie moved up to Kent College for Girls in Pembury, Kent. Her parents had worked hard and saved enough so that their beloved daughter could attend the exclusive £1,500-a-term school. Sophie was one of the few day girls in her year. An interdenominational Christian school which welcomes girls of all faiths, Kent College was founded in Folkestone over one hundred years ago by the Wesleyan Methodist Schools Association. It moved to Pembury in 1939.

The school offers a stunning environment in which to learn. Surrounded by beautiful green countryside, the fields are filled with animals and trees; the campus comprises an elegant Victorian manor house with a charming wooden interior while elsewhere there are purpose-built modern facilities, where the pupils live and study together.

It was here that Sophie developed the sporty side of her character. She excelled at team games, such as rounders, tennis, netball and hockey, and showed a great aptitude for athletics and swimming. The latter was a necessity since her father had also begun teaching Sophie to sail. It was not the only predominantly masculine sport in which she was involved: her school chaplain, Trevor Vickery also taught her the basics of boxing in the school gym. Such a strong early interest in sport translated itself into a life-long enjoyment of various outdoor activities, many of which she shares with her future husband. Not only was Prince Edward exceptionally bright in the classroom but he also excelled on the school playing fields, something of which his father, the Duke of Edinburgh, was incredibly proud.

At this time in her school career, Sophie showed a good deal of academic promise. Much to the delight of her parents, she had been seeded in the top set in her year and was in the Latin form, which was for the brighter girls. The not-so-bright girls were placed in the Domestic Science form. Although Sophie enjoyed working in the classroom, she hated exams. Her school reports show that she was very practical, good at Art and speaking French.

Sophie also sang in the school choir and some of her old school friends have commented that, 'She had a lovely voice and never suffered from stage fright, even when she had a solo to sing.' Standing up in front of people, performing, reciting and even acting came remarkably easily to Sophie. She volunteered for drama activities and had a minor part in a school production of *The Wizard of Oz*, and at the age of sixteen she won a song and dance part in the Cranbrook Operatic & Dramatic Society's version of *My Fair Lady*.

The previous year Sophie met her first boyfriend, David Kinder through her drama activities. They were both fifteen, and were introduced while doing workshop theatre productions at Tonbridge Boys' School in Kent. David was starring in his school's production of Edward Albee's satire, *The American Dream*, and both Sophie and her friend, Sarah Sienesi had successfully auditioned for parts. Sophie's and David's friendship soon blossomed into a romance. They enjoyed tennis together, but the relationship didn't last long. David, of course, remembers Sophie and speaks of her fondly. In what would prove to be a recurrent theme among Sophie's boyfriends, he particularly recalls the parties they attended together – many at his parents' home in Chislehurst, Kent.

Sophie, as David was the first to publicly note, was 'very popular with boys.' One schoolfriend recalled that: 'She was never short of a boyfriend.' No doubt her sporting activities and the unusual fact that she was taking boxing lessons made her seem almost exotic. Whatever it was that she possessed, it made her irresistible to the opposite sex. 'Even when she had a boyfriend,' said one of her friends, 'she still had all the other boys eating out of her hand. We'd all go green with envy.'

However, none of Sophie's antics were ever dangerous or offensive. Another friend remarked how, 'She was one of those genuinely nice girls who never got black marks. But she wasn't a goody-two-shoes either.' This is a view that is shared by another friend who commented that, 'She was an average student who was very pleasant. I never heard anyone say a bad word about her.'

By the time Sophie was sixteen she had displayed several qualities which would stand her in good stead for the rest of her life. She clearly had a knack for impressing people and winning them over. Sophie also demonstrated a single-minded commitment to winning that was almost frightening. Witness the fact that she is remembered by former school friends as a cheery, boisterous sort who became a 'total animal' anywhere near a hockey pitch.

Over: Sophie demonstrates her fearless qualities at Cowes.

'She was a real demon when armed with a hockey stick,' reported a school chum to the *Sun* newspaper after news of her attachment to Edward broke in 1994. 'Sophie wanted to win at all costs and God help anyone who tried to get in her way.' Another friend remarked, 'She was super-fit and could run like the wind. She was one of the few people I can remember who actually enjoyed their training. She was a real keep-fit addict who would try her hand at anything. We were all jealous because she could eat like a horse and it never showed.'

It takes a certain kind of single-minded determination to become as fit as Sophie was then. And it is clear that from a very early age Sophie Rhys-Jones was determined to find her metier, to excel, to make something of herself.

It was not entirely disingenuous of Sophie's parents to remark to the Press that, 'Sophie is a normal girl who has had a normal life. She grew up round here and attended local school, and did all the things that little girls do.' That is how they see it. They are justly proud of their daughter and expect nothing less of her than success in whatever she chooses to do.

And there lies the key to Sophie Rhys-Jones: she is her parents' daughter, imbued with their sense of right and wrong, filled with the notion of hard work allowing hard play, tempered with confidence. *Sophie*

Christopher Rhys-Jones encouraged Sophie's love of watersports.

Further Education, Boys & Beer

ophie began to lose interest in her studies just before taking her 'O'levels. Despite this, she still ended up with six passes, including Art and Religious Education. Sophie wasn't unduly concerned. She may not have had a clear and planned schedule for the rest of her life, but becoming an academic probably didn't figure on her list of things to do. The only thing of which she was certain was that she would leave the country and move to London.

Christopher and Mary pragmatically suggested that Sophie should have a practical skill of some kind to 'fall back on' if things ever became difficult for her. They had no real problem with their daughter's wish to fly the nest and see something more of the world, but at the same time they were acutely aware of the probability that at some point she would need to earn her own living. Arguing common sense, they persuaded Sophie to put her dreams on hold for two more years and, in September 1981, she enrolled on a two-year secretarial studies course at the West Kent College of Further Education in Tonbridge, to make sure – as her father put it – 'that she was qualified in something.'

Sophie's close college friend, Jo Last.

Usually Sophie would take the train from Paddock Wood station to college, undoubtedly dreaming of staying on the train to continue the journey on to London. Sometimes, though, her college friend, Jo Last would pick her up in her old brown Citroen 2CV (which she called Matilda). Chugging up to the gate of Homestead, Jo would toot on her horn and Sophie would invariably come running out, half-eating toast, with her bag and coat flapping behind her. At the time Jo lived in Goudhurst, about ten minutes from Brenchley. She now lives in America, where the *Sun* tracked her down and asked for her memories of a future English Duchess. Jo, like all Sophie's former friends and acquaintances, remembered her very well: 'She's funny, witty, smart, sweet but not stuck-up,' gushed Jo, continuing, 'Sophie is an extraordinary, normal and down-to-earth, decent girl.'

There are a number of almost contradictory compliments within those two sentences. Sophie manages to be 'extraordinary', yet 'normal'. She is clearly possessed of a sharp sense of humour, but 'not stuck-up'. Reading between the lines, one could suppose that Jo may have been a little in awe of her blonde chum.

Sophie (ringed, left) with a group of friends from her college days.

'She was tremendously open, warm, sweet and funny,' continued Jo. 'We poured out our hearts to each other from the start. That's what I remembered most about her. She was incredibly pretty, with great skin, a big smile and the same smart hairdo she has today.'

It was a golden time for Sophie and Jo at college. Anxious to avoid the possibility of a repeat exam performance, Sophie worked hard and not only took a secretarial course, but also found time to study 'O'-level Law and two 'A'-levels. 'I remember picking Sophie up on the morning of our English 'A'-level,' says Jo. 'We were both sitting in Matilda doing some last-minute revision. Suddenly, at exactly the same time, we both looked up, grinned at each other – and threw the notes through the sunroof. We started giggling uncontrollably and were laughing as we entered the exam room. She passed with flying colours – I flunked it.'

Not that Sophie just worked at college, of course. One of her former teachers, who taught her shorthand and typing, fifty-year-old Marion Vellino, spoke to the US magazine *People* saying, 'I was very fond of Sophie – she was a lively young lady.' Marion continued, perhaps unnecessarily, 'But if you had told me she was going to marry a prince, I would have said, "Pull the other one!" '

It was around this time, aged seventeen, that Sophie met her second 'serious' boyfriend, Rupert Scott-Mackie. He was the older brother of a school friend and had just started his job in the City working in insurance. Rupert, who still lived in Kent, met Sophie at a party and they began to see each other immediately. The relationship didn't last long, but Rupert still remembers Sophie: 'She was vivacious, very good-looking and had a particularly nice figure.' After a brief pause he added, almost wistfully, 'Unfortunately, we only went out briefly.'

When Sophie wasn't at college, her social life, like that of most students, revolved around the local pubs, including the impressive sixteenth-century Rose and Crown, its next door neighbour, The Bull and The Peacock, just outside the village. Sophie was well known as being something of a party girl in most of the village pubs. As a friend at the time said, 'She wasn't permissive, but she was fun-loving.'

Like many groups of local teenagers, Sophie's friends used to be very lively as they hung out in Brenchley's pubs and Sophie, often wearing her customary Puffa jacket and Hunter wellies, was the ringleader in their various night-time escapades. She was, by common consent, 'the life and soul of all their parties', of which there were many. 'They were a noisy, but fun crowd,' said a pub regular, adding 'they never caused any bother.' It has been remarked that Sophie could definitely hold her own with the crowd.

Recalling Sophie's drinking escapades at her brother, David's twenty-first birthday party, held in the Castle Hill pub in Brenchley, a former 'friend' said, 'She wanted to have a good time and didn't care about anything else.' Downing gin and tonics, she apparently had a good laugh at her brother, who was slightly under the weather. 'She could laugh at saucy jokes with any man, and certainly managed to hold her own in the drinking stakes,' said the former 'friend'.

The camaraderie built up on the many pub-raiding jaunts of Sophie's friends proved to be lasting. A consistent theme of her life so far has been Sophie's ability to remain friends with people that she may have physically, and even emotionally, moved away from. Even ex-boyfriends have remained close to her.

Not long after she split up with Rupert, Sophie enjoyed what she herself refers to as a 'fling' with computer wizard, John Blackman. They only went out briefly, but long after they stopped seeing each other romantically, 'Blackers' (as he was known) clubbed together with some of Sophie's other friends to give her a skiing holiday for her twenty-first birthday.

Blackers' friend told the *Sun*, 'Sophie is just like a sister to him now. They share a deep bond and he is possibly one of the only people she truly trusts. John, Sophie and a few of their other friends have formed a skiing party nearly every year since her twenty-first and she sees him regularly.'

After Blackers, Sophie dated her father's godson, Rupert Keane. Descended from an old Anglo-Irish family, both Sophie and Rupert's families seriously wondered whether they would marry and possibly even hoped that they would. After all, they had known each other since childhood. But it wasn't to be and, just like her relationship with Blackers, they split but subsequently became friends. During her two years at college, Sophie was keen to leave home and move to the City, which was only a tempting forty miles away. Bearing in mind her parent's concerns about her financial welfare, she knew that she needed to save up and so she took a job as a part-time waitress and barmaid in one of Brenchley's most popular local pubs, the Halfway House.

The Halfway House is just outside the village, hard on the road to Horsemonden. Warm and wooden, the pub itself has hardly changed since

The Halfway House, where Sophie worked as a part-time barmaid.

Sophie's early experience working in pubs proved very useful.

Sophie worked there over ten years ago and still serves traditional cask ales and filling pub lunches.

For the former ballet and dance student, the job represented another chance to entertain and perform. Sophie made a big impression on the customers. 'She was about eighteen at the time, very pleasant and attractive, and she always used to fill the pints up, which was unusual,' laughed one Halfway regular. 'She was a great girl to have behind the bar of your local, always chatting with the customers.'

The customers really appreciated all this. As one remarked, 'She was hard-working and charming. She really seemed to enjoy chatting to everyone who came in.' Another Brenchley resident told *People* magazine, 'She was a very attractive girl, I wished I was twenty years younger myself. And she pulled a good pint.'

Bar work must have been fun for Sophie while it lasted, but it was never meant to be for that long. By the end of her college course in 1983, she had worked hard enough at her studies, and in the aptly named Halfway House to have saved up enough money to move to London. But she didn't go alone. Sophie took a very important part of her Brenchley life with her: she arrived in the City with her oldest and best friend from her dance class days, Sarah Sienisi.

London Girl

Sophie was young, free and single, and the bright lights of the capital were at last within her determined grasp. She and Sarah Sienisi found themselves a cheap flatshare in Barons Court in West London, just minutes away from Queen's Tennis Club, where Sophie was later to meet Prince Edward. Armed with her newly acquired secretarial qualifications, she began job hunting and it wasn't long before she found work as a secretary for the Quentin Bell Organisation, a large PR firm based in London's Covent Garden.

This was her first taste of the PR world, where high-powered deals are done over expensive lunches and good communication skills are more important than an Oxford First. Sophie must quickly have realized that her own easy-going charm was a major asset in a PR career. First though, she needed to understand how the media world worked, so she moved on to Capital Radio, where she spent the next three 'wonderful' years learning everything she could about broadcasting.

It was an exhilarating time. Sophie was: 'brilliant fun – always laughing and joking,' according to one of her co-workers. She was extremely popular

Sophie, shown here on the St Moritz slopes, once worked as a skiing rep.

Sophie briefly dated music producer and keen sportsman, Andrew Parkinson, son of the famous TV presenter.

and, although working in a relatively lowly position as a secretary in the promotions department, soon became friends with Capital's biggest star, the TV and radio presenter, Chris Tarrant. As one colleague from Capital wryly put it: 'For ages there was a picture on the office noticeboard of Sophie asleep on a beach topless, with Chris Tarrant hovering over her. It disappeared the day the news broke that she was with Edward.'

It was during her three-year stint at Capital that Sophie was introduced to Prince Edward for the first time. The Prince was dating a friend of her's, and their meeting was brief and very casual. But although romance didn't spark on that occasion, perhaps Sophie did make a mental note about Edward's attractiveness – and eligibility. As one of her then boyfriends, Andrew Parkinson (TV presenter Michael Parkinson's son) remarked: 'Sophie was fairly enamoured of titles and stuff like that. She used to go to society balls and would stay at people's country houses. She loved to move in those circles.'

During the Capital years, Sophie's own romantic life was hectic enough without the added complication of dating a prince. She had several boyfriends, including Andrew Parkinson, who was a music producer and keen sportsman, and captained the Under-nineteen Berkshire cricket team. He was considered something of a catch by his Capital colleagues. 'Ours was never a serious relationship,' he said of Sophie, 'but I was attracted to her bubbly personality. She was very generous, honest and open, which is why I liked her.'

The couple only dated for about six weeks, then Andrew was replaced in Sophie's affections by Jeremy Barkley, whom she called 'Jez'. He came from Caversham, near Reading and ran an air-conditioning company. Jez was interested in cars and motoring, and was so fond of Sophie that he bought her first car, a 1967 Morris Minor. Their relationship lasted for some time, and who knows whether it was fondness or regret that made Sophie cry when she later traded in Jez's Morris for a new car?

Like many of her other boyfriends, Jeremy has only good things to say about the future royal bride: 'She is a fabulous girl and we are still friends. Sophie is one of those people it is a pleasure to have in your life – a very grown-up, fun-loving woman,' he says. One of her close friends said of Sophie: '[She's] sophisticated and understands what makes a relationship succeed. As a result, she has remained firm friends with most of the men she dated.' That's a hard act to pull off, especially for a young woman in her early twenties. It only goes to prove how mature Sophie already was.

Sophie was certainly grown-up enough to recognize that she needed a change. After three years' hard work at Capital, she realized that she had been neglecting the adventure-loving side of her personality. She wanted new challenges, to travel and see the world. But unlike many of the young, well-heeled friends with whom she hung around, Sophie also needed to earn her keep, so she put her mind and considerable talents into finding herself a job abroad.

It didn't take long. By December 1989, Sophie was off to Switzerland to work as a rep for the London-based ski company, Bladon Lines. Many girls of Sophie's age, experience and background become chalet girls. However, perhaps it was Sophie's evident communication and 'people' skills that got her instead a tougher and more senior position – that of managing the chalet girls in the exclusive ski resort of Crans-Montana in Switzerland.

Being a rep didn't mean that Sophie could enjoy the same style of living as the Bladon Lines' paying guests. In fact, she had only £65 a week to live on, plus a tiny rent-free apartment. Gareth Crump, now Bladon Lines' alpine manager, was a fellow rep at the time: 'Sophie always struck me as very capable,' he said. 'She was the kind of pretty girl all the male reps would congregate round.' Using the charm and wit that had stood her in such good stead in London, she undoubtedly managed to have fun. Many remember her as, 'the prettiest, wittiest woman around. She was great fun, the life and soul of every party.'

Crans-Montana, in the heart of the Swiss Alps, is an international ski resort famed for its lively nightlife. More James Bond than *The Sound of Music*, Crans appeals to an international crowd, who find traditional Swiss village charm as cloying as too much glühwein. Although the town has only 8,000 residents, there are over fifty restaurants and countless bars. But of course, eating and drinking weren't the only sources of entertainment on offer. Crans has almost enough international designer shops to rival Bond Street and, when off-duty and off-piste, Sophie could window shop to her heart's content.

However, Sophie never neglected her day duties. During the day the blue-eyed blonde would display an icy coolness when carrying out her work for the ski company. But her air of efficiency didn't distance her from the paying guests. 'They loved her,' said one rep. 'Sophie was enormous fun, great at meeting people and a dab hand on the cheese fondue.' Apparently, though, there was one thing at which Sophie wasn't so skilled: according to one colleague, her stem christies (a skiing technique) 'needed work'.

Although Sophie would not have realized it at the time, her job at Bladon Lines gave her a wonderful opportunity to hone her PR skills. As a chief rep in Crans, part of her job was to set up the entertainment for the guests. This included organizing the traditional après-ski fondue nights, as well as golf and ten-pin bowling. While it was not quite in the same league

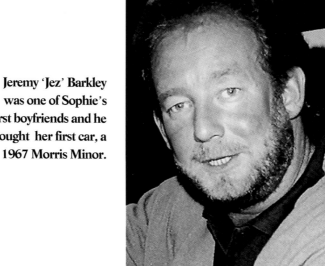

Jeremy 'Jez' Barkley was one of Sophie's first boyfriends and he bought her first car, a 1967 Morris Minor.

as some of Sophie's later ventures in PR, it was still experience and good practice none the less.

Although Sophie was never short of an escort to take her out, it was in Crans that she met her first real love. 'Unlike some of the girls, away from home for the first time, Sophie didn't succumb to the temptation to play the field of available men,' explained Gareth Crump. Instead, she started dating a tall, dark, handsome Australian ski instructor called Michael O'Neill. Deeply in love, and after only four months together in Switzerland, she and Michael moved to Sydney, Australia together. *Sophie*

Over: Sophie, spotted by the press whilst shopping with a friend near her home in West London.

Sophie's Big Adventure Down Under

Sydney is a big, exciting city, especially if you're in your early twenties and in search of fun. Sophie and Michael found themselves a little house in Paddington, one of the trendiest suburbs and a hang-out for Brits and backpackers stopping off for a few months on their round-the-world trips. Being a native Aussie, Michael knew his way round the city and showed Sophie the sights.

After a few happy months, however, their relationship came to an end. Although Michael was smitten with Sophie, she decided she simply wasn't ready to settle down to the comfortable lifestyle that Michael seemed to have planned out for them. Sophie wanted to enjoy her freedom and experience life – after all, she was thousands of miles from home with no restrictions or responsibilities. She wanted some fun.

So, instead of hopping on the first flight home once the relationship was over, Sophie decided to stay on in Australia by herself for a while. After a few weeks, she found a job working for courier company – Jet Services on Bowden Street in Alexandria, another Sydney suburb. Her former boss at Jet Services remembers her well and can't praise her enough: 'She seemed a

At weekends Sophie enjoyed yachting (and partying) on the Tasman Sea.

Sophie had a fantastic time in Australia and widened her circle of friends.

bright, bubbly girl, who was great fun.' And of course, he added: 'And she liked to party.'

There are always plenty of young English people either working in Australia or backpacking through the country. They tend to hang out in English-style pubs, such as the Lord Dudley and the London Tavern located in the city centre. Sophie had a fantastic time with the new friends she met there – a good mixture of Australian and English people, including a nightclub DJ known as 'Brown Bottle' (real name Andrew Hartley) and a fellow employee at Jet Services known as 'Spike' (a.k.a. Andy Cullity).

When she wasn't partying on the beach or lounging around in the sun, Sophie would often sit and drink champagne in one of the trendy oyster

Sophie (second left) with Eon Balmain and yachting companions.

bars in Circular Quay, overlooking Sydney Harbour. The Quay has incredible views of the Opera House, Harbour Bridge and the Botanical Gardens, and after a busy day at work, Sophie and her friends used to watch the sun set over the dramatic skyline.

Australia is heaven on earth for a sporty, outdoor girl like Sophie. As well as tennis, swimming and sailing, she joined a watersports club in Sydney and learnt subaqua diving. She loved to dive, exploring the underwater world and enjoying the solitude and peacefulness. At weekends Sophie used to escape the hubbub of the city by taking yacht trips on the Tasman Sea, the gulf of water between Australia and New Zealand. One of Sophie's regular yachting companions was graphic designer, Eon Balmain.

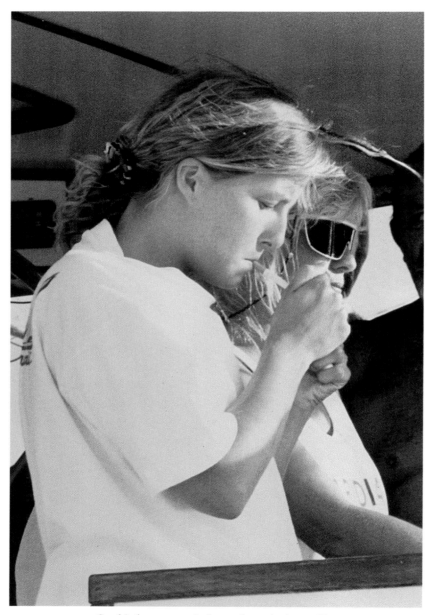

Sophie learnt true independence in Australia.

He was more than impressed with Sophie's ability to party: 'This was one girl who could hold her own with even the most hardened drinkers. We would start drinking early and keep going all day. But,' he added, 'while everyone else was all over the place, she always seemed totally in control.'

The group of friends would cruise around on the luxury yacht, Meridien, which had its own spa bath. According to Eon Balmain, Sophie never let her sense of decorum go astray: 'Though she loved to join in the spa with everyone and lark about, she always insisted that everyone kept their swimming costumes on.'

Sophie enjoyed the good life in Sydney for nearly a year, then decided to take time out and see some of the rest of Australia, travelling over New South Wales and north to Queensland and the Great Barrier Reef. Then, suddenly, she'd had enough. She wanted to go home. As one of her Australian companions from that time put it: 'It was as if Sophie had to get the party girl out of her system and was now ready to go out and face the real world.'

Australia had changed Sophie. After her relationship with Michael, there had been no significant men in her life, so she'd quickly had to learn how to look after herself, financially and emotionally. Far away from the support systems of family and home, she was forced to rely on herself for the first time in her life. She had always had plenty of determination and self-worth, but now she had found the strength of character that comes with true independence. Sophie had played and partied, and learned a lot, but now it was time to go home.

So, in 1992, Sophie got on a plane and left Australia and her old happy-go-lucky lifestyle behind her.

London Girl — Again

The last time Sophie had arrived in the capital with her old school friend, Sarah Sienisi, she was wide-eyed and innocent. This time, aged twenty-seven, she was much more ambitious and focused. As always with Sophie, the first step was to find herself a job. Preferably it would be one that would give her the opportunity not only to earn good money, but also to use her considerable 'people skills' and organizational flair. She found the ideal position as an assistant to the events organizer for the Macmillan Nurses Cancer Relief Fund. The annual salary of £12,000 a year was a vast improvement on the £65-a-week she had earned as a travel rep in Crans.

The Macmillan Nurses Cancer Relief Fund is a national charity devoted to caring for people with cancer from diagnosis, a cause that must have been close to her heart as her grandmother died of the disease when Sophie was eighteen. Macmillan nurses are cancer specialists and most of them are employed by the NHS to treat and care solely for cancer patients.

Three years before Sophie's arrival at the charity, £2.5 million had been invested towards increasing the number of Macmillan nurses nationwide.

Sophie leaves her flat in Kensington (June 1995).

Sophie in Knightsbridge, London (above) and with Frank Sidebottom in Manchester (below).

Sophie threw herself into the job with enormous enthusiasm and is remembered by colleagues for having 'boundless energy' and 'being full of life, inspiring everyone around her.' During her time there she worked on a memorable Easter Bunny campaign. Posters of rabbits in green bow-ties holding empty egg baskets were accompanied by the slogan 'You can't put too many eggs in this basket'. The public was asked to buy egg stickers at 20p- a-throw for the Appeal. It was a lovely poster, with the bunnies peering into the basket. 'She oversaw all the artwork,' muses Jill Phillips, national promotions manager at Macmillan. The promotional campaign brought in about £15,000 (*The Times*, December 1993).

When she left, she stayed in touch with the charity by joining the young appeals fundraising committee. 'I did it because they're such a nice bunch of people and the events are great fun,' Sophie explained. 'I also think that the Macmillan nurses are fantastic. I've had cause to contact them in the past on behalf of friends with cancer.'

Since then Sophie has helped other cancer charities, including The Haven Trust which 'aims to supplement the care that hospitals give by providing all-round care to cancer sufferers in one place', as she explained to *Hello!* magazine in 1997. (Sophie asked *Hello!* to donate her substantial interview fee to The Haven Trust.)

On her return to London Sophie was working very hard, but still made time to meet old friends, and make some new ones. There were quite a few men who were interested in the vivacious blonde, including her dentist, Tim King. Their 'fling', as Sophie put it, was short-lived, but obviously good fun. The handsome dentist was a flying enthusiast and the couple often spent weekends hopping over the Channel to Le Touquet in France, or further down the coast to Spain. Sometimes they would go for romantic skiing weekends to Andorra. (Once they were stuck there for four extra days because of bad weather. Sophie didn't complain, though. She loved to ski and it wasn't her fault that she had to take some unexpected time off work.) After a few months, Sophie and Tim parted amicably, and she stayed on as a patient at his King's Road surgery in Chelsea for some time afterwards.

Sophie still occasionally popped down to visit her friends in Brenchley, especially when there was a party going on. At one such karaoke party that took place in Sussex, friends remember her letting her hair down and singing 'You're the One That I Want' and 'Summer Nights' from the hit musical *Grease* with great energy.

Back in the workplace, Sophie's talent for PR hadn't gone unnoticed. After a year at the Macmillan Nurses Cancer Relief Fund she was headhunted by MacLaurin Communication and Media (known as MCM), a West London public relations company run by Brian MacLaurin. MacLaurin, a dynamic, handsome Scotsman, hired Sophie on the recommendation of the former head of promotions at Capital Radio, Anita Hamilton, because she was 'lively, knowledgeable and bright.'

MCM had a large and varied client list including Thomas the Tank Engine, Noel Edmonds, Mr Blobby, Mobil Oil, Heart FM and her old friend from her days at Capital Radio, the DJ and television personality, Chris Tarrant. Sophie worked on most of these accounts though never, as Brian MacLaurin was later to point out, on the Mr Blobby account. (However, this didn't stop newspapers all over the country from writing headlines along the lines of 'Edward falls for Blobby's girl' when the story of her romance with Edward first became public.)

Colleagues at MCM said that Sophie was 'charming and very efficient' and exceptionally good at her job. Her annual salary, increased by £14,000, reflected the confidence that the company had in her. Meanwhile, she moved to a slightly larger flat in West London to live with her friend, Ulrike von Herwarth.

Ulrike, a stunning blonde and former air stewardess, was later to prove a great help to Sophie when it came to understanding Royal protocol and etiquette, as she herself comes from a very distinguished family. She is related to the Marquess of Conyngham and the first German ambassador to the Court of St James after the war.

If Sophie didn't know of her new flatmate's royal pedigree before, she was about to find out. And how.

The block of flats in West Kensington, where Sophie once lived.

Someday My Prince Will Come

I t was in August 1993 while working at MCM that, by an extraordinary set of circumstances, Sophie met her prince again, and this time the meeting was to transform her life. On that fateful morning at Queen's Club, Edward was actually scheduled to pose for a press call with another athletic blonde – the former tennis player and *Question of Sport* presenter, Sue Barker.

Some time before that Queen's Club event, Sophie's boss, Brian MacLaurin, had been invited to Buckingham Palace to give PR advice about raising public awareness of the Prince Edward Challenge, which was aiming to raise money for local charities via local radio. The Prince had the idea of getting young people from all over the country to take on various sponsored endurance tests.

As his own contribution to the Challenge, Edward decided to play a twelve-hour real tennis marathon against a rolling team of opponents. Even though there were reports that the Palace hated the idea, it was eventually passed, and Sue Barker was duly booked to pose alongside Edward for the publicity photographs.

The Prince Edward Challenge photocall that was to change Sophie's life.

Sophie and Edward avoided the Press for as long as possible.

However, at the eleventh hour, Ms Barker had to pull out. Brian MacLaurin thought fast, and turned to Sophie. (As he later put it: 'I played Cupid.') It was all a huge rush. One person who was in MCM that day explained: 'Brian came out of his office and said, "Sophie, in the car." ' So Sophie went home with him and grabbed a black leotard from her flat, then raced over to the photoshoot.

'I asked the Prince if he would mind doing the pictures with Sophie instead,' remembered MacLaurin. 'He rocked on his heels, then had a peek at Sophie and said that would be fine.'

One perceptive onlooker who was present at the shoot was amused at Edward's obvious interest in Sophie. 'He kept giving her sideways looks as she did these quick changes, whipping on the first T-shirt with the logo of a radio station, whipping it off again, and so on.' However, the attraction wasn't generally apparent. 'Nobody knew that there was an attraction between them that day,' recalls real tennis champion, Sally Jones, one of the Prince's opponents for his marathon stint. 'But Edward always had an eye for a bright girl – and Sophie is bright, sparky and fun.'

Sophie followed the instructions from the photographer and did exactly what she was told. By putting a jaunty arm on Edward's shoulder for the photocall, she was flying in the face of Royal protocol, but Edward seemed to love it. 'She was totally uninhibited,' said MacLaurin. 'She treated him as a perfectly normal person and I suspect that was the initial appeal.' Of course, that relaxed, sexy photograph was the one that soon made an appearance in all the newspapers, and everybody wanted to know 'Who's that girl?' Perhaps she had an idea that her cheeky move in making physical contact with Edward for publicity photographs would cause some ripples in the media – after all, she was in PR and the idea was to get as much press coverage for the event as possible – but it's unlikely that Sophie knew exactly how much that one pose would affect her life. Quite simply, it would never be the same again.

The couple met a few days later when Sophie travelled with her boss to Buckingham Palace for a breakfast meeting to discuss the next stage of their publicity campaign. However, despite the fact that Edward had secretly asked Sophie for her phone number at the Queen's Club photocall, the couple didn't actually go on a date together until a few weeks later. 'Nothing happened for a while,' said Brian MacLaurin, 'until Edward held a VIP function for his charity. I couldn't go, so passed my invitation on to Sophie. It was that night he first asked her out.'

In November 1993, about six weeks after their first date, Edward had to fly off to Australia on behalf of the Duke of Edinburgh Award Scheme. Parting proved to be such sweet sorrow for him, it seems. He missed Sophie enough to phone her nearly every day, using a pseudonym (either 'Richard' or 'Gus') whenever he called her at the office.

Both Edward and Sophie went to enormous lengths to keep their romance secret. Whenever he picked up Sophie from her West London flat, he would hide in the car while he sent his detective, Steve to ring the doorbell and escort her to the car. Although they would go out as a happy threesome (Sophie, Edward and the detective), more often than not the couple would stay in and eat together. Brian MacLaurin knew of the relationship, but was impressed by Sophie's discretion. 'She didn't tell a solitary soul,' he said. 'She became a very private person. She was so discreet it was unbelievable. It was really clever of her.'

And it must have added spice to the relationship, too, to keep it hidden so carefully from the Press, public and friends. After all, there's nothing so exciting as a clandestine relationship. And this friendship was one of the biggest secrets in town.

Sophie and Prince Edward attend the Royal Squadron Ball at Cowes.

The Discovery

I n the 1990s it proved impossible for a public personality to keep a secret. The media (as it never ceased to inform us) would have to reveal any secrets that were in the public's interest. Therefore, it was only a matter of time before Edward and Sophie would be discovered. The fact that Edward managed to keep their relationship secret for three months was a great achievement and a testament to the loyalty and discretion of their friends. However, unfortunately for the couple, it was Andrew Morton who broke the news late in December 1993. The Royal family were doubly distressed by the fact that Morton had breached the wall of silence around the couple, since he had been the author of a controversial biography of Diana, Princess of Wales, which had caused both the Queen and Prince Charles some distress.

As with the Diana biography, Morton would not reveal the source of his information to Sophie, when he presented her with her first taste of press intrusion - and it wasn't going to be the last time.

It was a Friday afternoon in the West End of London, just a week before Christmas. The MCM staff were gearing up for the weekend, packing up

The late Diana, Princess of Wales, once lived in the same building as Sophie.

their desks and making those last-minute phonecalls before heading off to the nearest pub for an end-of-the-week drink. However, unseen by the security guards and front reception desk, Morton walked right up to Sophie's desk, where she was busy typing away at her computer. As she looked up, he confronted her with a smile, saying: 'May I be the first to call you Your Royal Highness, the Duchess of Cambridge?'

In that heart-stopping moment Sophie understood that the game was up. Someone had told Morton about herself and Edward but, worse still, he was implying that they were about to get married. Sophie sat behind her desk, shaking like a leaf, blushing furiously as Morton reeled off the times of her meetings with the Prince in great detail. After what must have seemed an age, but was less than two minutes, Brian MacLaurin ran over to protect Sophie, telling Morton, 'You're not going to gain anything by giving Sophie this hassle', and he whisked her off into the boardroom. There Brian calmed Sophie down and explained to her that she had to deal with Morton, and that, most importantly, she needed to answer him. After all, he reminded her, this job had given her an extensive training in dealing with sticky situations, although admittedly few were as awkward as this.

Re-entering her office with a slightly pale face, she issued the journalist with a brief statement: 'Prince Edward and I are good friends and we work together. He is a private person and so am I. I have nothing more to add.'

With that, Brian bustled Sophie out of the building, put her in the back of his silver Mazda, and the two of them sped off. Morton had his story and it wouldn't be long before the rest of the papers had the same.

Within an hour of Morton entering the MCM building, Sophie and Brian had contacted Edward, who took charge of the situation. She stopped off at her Earls Court flat – which, in a strange coincidence, happened to be within the same block of flats in which Princess Diana lived before her engagement to Prince Charles – and picked up three suitcases before being whisked off to the sanctuary of Windsor Castle.

Protected and feeling safe with Edward in Windsor, Sophie didn't have to worry about a thing. He took complete control of the situation. In a somewhat unusual step, but then again, protocol had never been clearly defined when it came to Royal romantic privacy, Edward took it upon

Comparisons with Diana were inevitable after the discovery.

Prince Edward with the late Diana, Princess of Wales.

himself to deny that there was about to be an engagement. He pleaded with the gathered press to leave him alone so that he could develop a relationship with Sophie in his own time and at his own pace.

In a remarkable attempt to get the Press off their backs, the Prince personally addressed all the Fleet Street editors on notepaper from his Ardent Productions Limited company. Signing it 'Edward Windsor', he ruled out any marriage plans, stating that, 'If the situation changes we will let you know in a proper and formal manner.' The letter continued, 'I am very conscious that other members of my immediate family have been subjected to similar attention and it has not been at all beneficial to their relationships. Therefore, please will you call an end to your harassment of Sophie and me, and allow us to try and carry on our lives as normal. Please will you consider our case seriously, especially as it is Christmas and the season of goodwill.'

According to Ingrid Seward, editor of *Majesty* magazine, 'Edward said that the decision to ask the media to be left alone to conduct his romance with Sophie hadn't been easy. Various commentators started to say things like 'People in glass houses shouldn't throw bricks', which [he] never understood, because [he] hadn't thrown any bricks. [He] had just said, "Lay off, please." '

Edward's letter helped to take some of the heat away from the couple at the time, though in the long run it didn't make an enormous amount of difference. It did, however, make the Press realize that he was deadly serious about his intent and that they ought to back off somewhat. Clearly, Edward isn't the kind of man who likes being backed into a corner, especially not by the media, and when it comes to his personal life, he is fiercely protective. When people start interfering, as the editors learnt, he gets very defensive.

Perhaps in the spirit of seasonal goodwill the couple found some space to themselves away from prying telephoto lenses. However, the newspapers continued to bandy around the word 'engagement'. The couple were supported by well-meaning relatives, such as Sophie's aunt, Jill Rhys-Jones, who told the Press, 'They have a chance to make a real go of it. She is gregarious, vivacious, a sweetie. We think she is a poppet and have our fingers crossed. It would be lovely if they stood a chance and we would be delighted if they could make it in the present climate.'

Sophie's boss, Brian MacLaurin, a dab hand at dealing with the Press, took it upon himself to protect Sophie. Speaking publicly, he tried to deflect the question of marriage. In an interview given to the Press, he said, 'I have spoken to Sophie and to Edward, and the key message from them is "Give us a break." Their relationship is just three months old in terms of [being] good friends, and there is presumably a long way to go.'

Unsurprisingly, there were plenty of people ready to leap to Sophie's defence, to try and deflect media attention away from the couple. Her father, Christopher, tried to calm a highly speculative press by saying, 'We don't know much about their relationship, only that they met in August. Sophie is very happy at the moment but upset about all the media attention. She just wants a quiet life.'

It's impossible to know how much time, if any, Sophie had dedicated to thinking about the peculiar type of fame bestowed upon those fortunate few who become publicly involved with a member of the Royal family. And it's unlikely that a woman as informed in the ways of the media as Sophie would not have an idea of what was to come her way. The world had watched every faltering step taken by Diana, Princess of Wales, as she developed from shy au pair to blushing Royal bride and onto the covers of the world's most prestigious and popular newspapers and magazines. Perhaps at some time in the three relatively quiet months of the couple's courtship, Sophie pondered on the day that she would have the photographers of the world's press on her doorstep, and how she would handle it.

Possibly as a result of her now more public appearances, Sophie had her shoulder-length blonde hair chopped off in favour of a shorter, more coiffed look. Unfortunately, this action resulted in a myriad of ridiculous articles in which Royal watchers, so-called fashion 'experts' and gossip columnists speculated about the new, but striking similarity between Sophie and Diana.

The pressure must have been intense for the young PR executive, as Sophie herself hinted at: 'It is scary when suddenly you are bang in the middle of it all,' she stated, adding with great understatement, 'It does take a while to get used to, in terms of starting a new relationship as well.' Any doubts that Edward or her closest friends and family may have had about Sophie's ability to handle events must have been instantly dispelled on hearing that statement. Contained within it are some of Sophie's best qualities: humour, strength and common sense.

Naturally enough, around this time genealogists started to take an interest in Sophie's heritage. It was through their work that she discovered her Welsh and Irish roots, and the fact that the Rhys-Jones's weren't quite the commoners that everyone, including themselves, had thought. *Debretts Peerage* unearthed the little-known fact that through her father's grandmother, Sophie was, in fact, the sixth cousin once removed of the eleventh Viscount Molesworth, a seventeenth-century diplomat with links to the Stuart kings of Scotland and the Queen Mother. Furthermore, Sophie could now claim that the previous artistic and theatrical streaks that she had demonstrated as a child could have come from her fifth cousins – the screen legends, Olivia de Havilland and her sister Joan Fontaine. No one was more surprised at these revelations than Sophie herself, who reportedly shared a laugh over it all with her old friends.

The Palace, meanwhile, tried to help the newest recruit to the ranks as much as possible, by sending her a letter with a list of instructions of how one is supposed to behave as a Royal, together with handy hints to avoid scandal. After the embarrassing public debacles of Squidgygate and the Charles and Camilla tapes (made public in August 1992 and January 1993 respectively), in which private personal telephone calls made by Charles, Diana and Camilla Parker-Bowles, the Prince of Wales' mistress had been published by tabloid newspapers around the world, the last thing the Palace wanted was another *cause célèbre* in their camp.

Thus the letter from the senior court official, which was marked 'private and confidential', concerned itself primarily with her use of the telephone. She was advised not to use a hands-free set as they were the easiest ones to listen in on, but to get a digital mobile phone instead.

Her training as a Royal-in-waiting had truly begun.

Meeting the In-Laws

With Sophie's acceptance into the Royal fold now public knowledge, she was scheduled to make her first official appearance with the Royal Family. Sophie was invited to join them for their traditional Sandringham house party on New Year's Eve, 1993. This, by all accounts, is a daunting occasion for anyone, least of all a newcomer to the Royal circle.

Now a nice girl from West Kensington might have a wardrobe to wear to a friend's dinner party or even a ball or two, but a weekend with the Royals? This was another prospect entirely and regular High Street shops really wouldn't do at all. Weekend visitors to Sandringham find themselves changing clothes at least four or five times a day, depending on whether they are attending a shoot, riding or sitting down to black-tie evening meals. Sophie was lucky enough to have friends on whom she could rely for advice and tips on what to wear and how to behave. Some even lent her clothes; a sensible green, waxed Barbour jacket, plus suitable hats and dresses.

Sophie, of course, passed her 'Royal Test' with flying colours. The girl from Brenchley made a good impression on both the Queen and Prince

Sophie, Princess Margaret and Edward at Sandringham.

Sophie and Prince Edward on board the Royal yacht Britannia at Cowes.

Philip, with the Queen in particular taking to Sophie's straight-talking approach. One famous quote attributed to the Queen about Sophie is that, 'You wouldn't notice her in a crowd.' While at first this comment might be seen as dismissive, it was in fact a compliment. Sophie had clearly earned the Queen's approval, impressing her by being the kind of girl who wouldn't rock the boat – unlike Diana. If it hadn't been so prior to this, it certainly was by now very important to the Queen that any new relationships formed by her children should prove stable.

The proof of the Queen's approval of Sophie was immediately made clear when she invited Sophie's parents to Sandringham a few days into the New Year. It must have been an incredibly exciting but daunting prospect for the Rhys-Jones. Sophie's father, Christopher was moved to remark, not quite correctly, 'Let's face it, the Royal Family and the Rhys-Jones are a world apart.' There may once have been a world of difference separating the Windsor and the Rhys-Jones families, but their daughter had changed that for ever.

If Sophie had ever felt at all removed from Edward and his family, she didn't show it. When the holidays were finally over, she returned to work and, being Sophie, didn't allow the Royal association outwardly to affect her at all. Turning up with Edward to a real tennis event in mid-January at Hampton Court, she asked people, 'What can I do to help? Can I do the washing up?'

A matter of mere weeks later Sophie was hostess for a dinner party thrown by the Prince at the Palace for several hundred of their friends and supporters of Edward's Summer Challenge Charity. Observers noted that although she may have been quite nervous at first, by the time the main course had arrived, Sophie seemed totally at home.

When the couple made their second major public outing together, their roles in public seemed set. Sophie, accompanying Edward to a charity tennis tournament for the Lord Taverners charity, of which Edward is the president, was busy at work while he played in the competition. In fact, she worked so hard, it was reported, that she didn't have much time to watch Edward play.

Acutely aware that her every move was being watched, Sophie knew that not only what she did, but also what she looked like, would now matter far more than ever before. Remarking on a subtle change of style, one of her friends stated, 'She immediately became very conservative in what she wore and appeared to take on the Royal look straight away. Her skirts got longer and tweedier.'

That this quote became public demonstrated precisely why Sophie altered her appearance. Clothes and grooming are the two areas that young modern Royals will be judged on in print. Unlike the other two Royal partners, Princess Diana and the Duchess of York, Sophie didn't have the kind of finances that could support a high-maintenance wardrobe. However, being sensible and responsible, she resisted the pressure to live beyond her means and, for the very public affair of Edward's thirtieth birthday party at the Savoy Hotel in London, she wore a £300 shift dress. Though this might seem expensive to some, in Royal circles it was decidedly cheap. Yet, of course, she carried it off with panache and style, managing to impress upon the privileged few, among whose circles she now moved, that she had style and also to demonstrate to her old friends that she hadn't let things go to her head.

A month later, at the Suffolk wedding of Lord Ivar Mountbatten, Sophie wore a red Chinese-style jacket and a long black skirt split at the front to mid-thigh. Naturally, the choice of designer was a topic of debate. Some claimed that her clothes were from the High Street shop, Karen Millen, but others weren't so sure. Either way, everyone agreed that she looked radiant. (Later in the year, when the couple attended Lady Sarah Armstrong-Jones's wedding to Daniel Chatto, Sophie had stepped up a gear; she dazzled in a grey morning coat and cream skirt by the designer, Tomasz Starzewski.)

The wedding itself was a very Royal occasion. Lord Ivar's marriage to Penny Thompson had great social significance: not only did Ivar Mountbatten go to school with Prince Edward but they are both great-nephews of Earl Mountbatten of Burma (who was killed by the IRA in 1979). Furthermore, his father was best man at the Queen's marriage to Prince Philip.

During the ceremony, held in Clare Church, Suffolk, Sophie was seated between the Queen's sister Margaret and Prince Edward, and later watched as the Prince read one of the lessons, St Paul's Epistle to the Corinthians. Being sensitive and media-aware, Edward and Sophie were very careful not to draw too much attention to their relationship, which would detract from the happy couple's big day. They certainly didn't hold hands, but guests who attended the wedding could tell that they were obviously relaxed and happy with one another.

Edward and Sophie knew that pictures of the two of them doing anything intimate, even giving each other a peck on the cheek, would make front-page news around the world. This fact was clearly demonstrated when five tabloids published photographs of them kissing in the grounds of the Balmoral Estate. Edward was livid. The pictures had been taken using a long-range zoom lens and it was a direct invasion of privacy. He immediately contacted the Press Complaints Commission to appeal that his privacy was being compromised. His complaint was upheld and the newspapers involved apologized. Edward and Sophie thought that it might be the last instance they would have to face for a while. So it proved, but not for long.

Sophie passed her Royal Test with flying colours.

HM The Queen Mother greets Sophie at Scrabster, Scotland.

Still desperate for a story on the couple, journalists used to trail Sophie around wherever she went. Continuous digging by journalists meant that it was soon discovered that she would often stay overnight at Edward's second floor apartment in Buckingham Palace. Some press photographers had noticed her driving through the Palace gates in her blue Ford Fiesta in the early hours of the morning.

This knowledge led to several photographers waiting outside the Palace throughout the night to see if and when Sophie would leave. They were rewarded for their patience at 8 a.m., when Sophie was seen chatting to a security guard, throwing her overnight bag into the car and then driving off. By the next morning, pictures of her leaving the Palace were all over the newspapers.

Despite what could easily have become another setback in their relationship, both Sophie and Edward resolved not to be intimidated at all by the Press. Only a few days later, Sophie was photographed leaving the Palace again. Soon enough, everyone got bored of doorstepping the Palace. The couple were left in peace and Sophie was allowed to come and go as she pleased. Not for the last time, Sophie had altered Palace protocol and done it with little pain to the Royal family. Previous Royal partners waited until they were formally engaged before staying with their fiancés, and even then the utmost discretion was required.

Not that media attention dissipated. Only a few days after the Palace pictures had appeared in the Press, Sophie attended her friend, Geraldine Turner's wedding in secret – or so she thought. As she arrived at Fulford, near York, she spotted the photographers. Showing no signs of anger, she asked, 'How on earth did you know I was here? Did you follow me up from London?'

If there had been any truth at all in the rumours circulating at the time that the couple would become formally engaged, it was reasoned by Royal watchers that they would wait until after the twenty-fifth anniversary of Charles's investiture as Prince of Wales on 1 July 1994. This gave them some breathing space at least and meant that they could go about their business unhampered by any intrusive questions about their impending nuptials.

For the couple's first anniversary Edward, in a show of great affection, gave Sophie a four-inch high, £12,000 Teddy brooch. Sophie was seen wearing it as she left her office. Beaming, she turned to the assembled press and said, 'Isn't it lovely? I want to wear it all the time.'

As if the gift had made their relationship more real, little by little, Sophie started to appear in public with her new boyfriend more and more, accompanying him on several semi-official Royal outings. Edward guided Sophie gently through one of her first Royal adventures at Cowes Week in August 1994. He sent her a letter outlining precise instructions on how to get there, what to wear and even included a guest list of who would be on board the Royal yacht. Demonstrating the sense of humour that the pair shared, he finished the letter, 'If you have any questions or problems, please call. I think you know where you can get hold of me.'

Cowes is a great tradition for the Royals. For the past thirty years, the Duke of Edinburgh has hosted a Cowes Week party aboard his yacht, which is moored offshore from the Royal Squadron building on the Isle of Wight.

Sophie was seen relaxing with the Royals, playing deck tennis on board the Royal Yacht Britannia and then later, in front of the Press, bravely taking water-skiing lessons and sailing with the Prince. During the water-skiing lesson she fell off her skis and managed to get her towrope tangled up in the speedboat's propellers. Peter Phillips, the sixteen-year-old son of the Princess Royal, repeatedly dived into the water to try to untangle the propellers, but to no avail. Sophie was forced to ask the watching press photographers to help her. She then decided to have a windsurfing lesson, almost as disastrously, but as she began to slip off the board into the sea, she laughed.

That night, as tradition demands, the couple turned up together at the Royal Yacht Squadron Ball. It was clear from the moment they arrived and Sophie turned heads with her stunning dress, that they were happy to be together and to be seen together. They danced cheek-to-cheek to Gloria Gaynor's 'I Will Survive' and Cher's 'Shoop, Shoop Song', appearing to all the world like any other young couple in love.

According to one of Sophie's friends at the time, Edward took great care to make sure that Sophie didn't feel overwhelmed by all the attention. 'Sophie said he would call to make sure she hadn't had problems after she went out in public,' said Julie Ledger to *People* magazine. 'That's one of the things I think will make the relationship succeed – they have a good friendship, and they talk.'

By this time, when they were together the couple spent their weekends at Windsor Castle; this was one of the few places where they could be truly private. It was obvious that the Queen liked Sophie and, more importantly, approved of her. Sophie always had the use of her own room at Windsor and, after spending a little more time there, began to feel at ease with the Royal family, learning the correct etiquette, speaking when spoken to and keeping an appropriate distance. In typical Sophie style, she told a friend how to survive lunches at Windsor with the Queen: 'It's just like being at school. If you think of the Queen as the headmistress you can't go far wrong.'

As the year ended, Sophie and Edward were very much together, deeply in love, but still feeling their way together. Although seemingly at ease when in the public view with the Royals, Sophie still spent plenty of time away from them, working and enjoying life much as she always did. The strain of being a Royal twenty-four hours a day was quite possibly still a daunting prospect for her.

Again in 1994, Sophie attended the New Year's celebrations at Sandringham. After the traditional church service, the Royal Family went for a walkabout to meet the public. However, after catching sight of the 2,500-strong crowd, seemingly all desperate to catch a glimpse of Edward's new girlfriend, Sophie froze. She simply couldn't go out and face them. Instead, she slipped back into the church and out through a back door.

Sophie

Over: Sophie and Edward enjoy Palace life together.

To Be, Or Not To Be?

Edward and Sophie had spent the previous year avoiding all and any talk of an engagement. But after two years of courtship, the romance was sure to be made official and the couple were finally going to get engaged – or so went the popular rumour on Fleet Street as the New Year dawned, although not for long.

The reason was quite simple: Charles and Diana. The feuding Royal couple were becoming almost full-time headline news. All the world knew about and was discussing their marital problems. Sophie and Edward were astute enough to realize that any engagement announcement would be seen as an attempt to deflect the media's interest in Prince Charles's crumbling marriage. Edward, ever-protective of his own and Sophie's privacy, certainly didn't want to do anything that would encourage cynics to suggest that their marriage was nothing more than a Royal PR ploy.

Not that, according to certain 'sources', the couple hadn't talked privately of an engagement. To her great credit, Sophie controlled any urge she might have had to tell people of their plans, whether they involved marriage or not.

On board Britannia, Prince Philip clearly shows his support for Sophie.

Edward was perhaps more wary of public commitment than Sophie. One friend commented that, 'The problems with Diana and Fergie have made the Prince rather introspective about his own relationship. He tries to distance himself from the troubles plaguing the Royal family.'

By February, Edward was keen to get away from the British press scrum and spend some quality time with Sophie, so they went off skiing to St Moritz in Switzerland. Unfortunately, the Press followed them. Sophie was photographed enjoying her first snowboard lessons. Unlike her windsurfing class at Cowes two years previously, she acquitted herself with skill and grace, and seemed to enjoy herself immensely.

In what was to become normal Royal and Press behaviour, the couple allowed pictures to be taken during their days on the piste, and in return they were left alone in the evenings. Throughout the day, they were part of an official Royal skiing trip, with all that involves – guides, protection officers and several friends. Sophie and Edward didn't mind having so many people around them, but it was quite evident that they would like to spend some time alone together. They were clearly very much in love: Sophie was

Sophie joins in Edward's official duties.

always slipping her arm around Edward when she thought no one was looking. Despite that, the holiday was a success on all counts. The Press had their photographs and stories, Sophie and Edward enjoyed themselves – and there was no mention of a Royal wedding to deflect attention from the Windsors' woes.

On their return to London, they both went back to work. Edward travelled to Canada as part of his official duties for the Commonwealth Games. He missed Sophie so much that, though only away for a week, he sent her a postcard telling her how happy he was that he would soon be able to see her again, finishing it, 'with masses of love'.

On his return, their relationship stepped up a gear and Sophie made some important life changes. She negotiated a four-day working week at MCM, leaving her Fridays free for long weekends away with Edward. Together, the couple would escape to Windsor, Sandringham or Balmoral, finally getting the peace and privacy that they so craved and needed, if their relationship was to deepen. Spending many weekends with the Windsors, Sophie was also getting to know the Royal family extremely well.

So smooth was Sophie's integration into Royal circles that Princess Diana is reported to have asked, 'Why is she getting such an easy ride?' The answer, of course, was that Sophie and Edward rarely sought the spotlight themselves. Furthermore, the Palace had learnt lessons from previous mistakes. Sophie had the freedom to slip in and out of the Palace and learn Royal protocol in a relaxed environment with Edward her willing tutor.

Sophie also benefited from having an extremely discreet and trustworthy group of old friends. When not spending summer weekends with Edward, Sophie was most likely to be found in the Devonshire village of Stoke Fleming near Dartmouth. Sophie and her London gang often spent long weekends there during the village cricket season to escape the hustle and bustle of London.

The core of the clique are the five Lloyd-Edwards sisters – Sian, Ceri, Gwen, Broni and Beth – all of whom Sophie had known since 1984, when she met them on holiday in Stoke Fleming. The sisters struck up an immediate bond with the young Sophie when they realized that she shared two of their passions: sailing and cricket. With this crowd Sophie could relax and talk about anything – Edward, work, life and love – without any fear of her confidences being betrayed.

When, as she still does, Sophie joins the sisters for their house parties in Devon, there are usually at least twenty people present, including old boyfriends, the girls' parents and neighbours. They all pitch in, cooking, cleaning and, by common agreement, having a great time. Everyone in the Stoke Fleming set agrees that Sophie hasn't changed at all since her romance with Edward began. As if to an agreed party line, they chant the same mantra: that she's still the friendly, kind and nice person she always was. 'Sophie's a wonderful girl,' said one of the Lloyd-Edwards sisters, 'and a very natural person who takes one thing at a time in a perfectly calm and collected manner.'

The weekends have a familiar comforting pattern for Sophie: the fun begins with drinks at the Green Dragon pub on Friday night, and usually carries on with a swim and sunbathe on Saturday. Sunday is taken up with cricket; the boys playing, the girls watching. At night the group settles down to devour a huge meal cooked by the girls. This ritual has been going on since the late 1980s and was first started by Sophie's old boyfriend, John Blackman (Blackers).

Over: Sophie and Edward share the same enthusiasm for outdoor pursuits.

81

The easy atmosphere and strong bond of trust between the group also meant that Sophie felt confident enough to bring Edward along to some of their dinner parties in London. Slowly, Edward and Sophie were building up a network of friends among whom they felt at ease. Both were trying, in very difficult circumstances, to enjoy as 'normal' a relationship as possible.

Just before Christmas, Sophie made her second big work decision of the year and left MCM to go freelance. It was a brave and necessary move. By quitting her job, she hoped to avoid any embarrassment or conflict that her PR role might have brought to the Royal Family.

Brian MacLaurin, her boss at MCM, sent a memo to the staff saying it had 'become increasingly difficult for Sophie to operate in the frontline'. Echoing Brian's statement, Sophie herself told the staff that, 'I have to retreat from frontline PR. It has presented me with various compromising situations on a personal level.' The company were sad to lose her. Not only did her Royal associations bring extra publicity for MCM but, of course, Sophie was popular and good at her job.

That weekend, Sophie and Edward took a romantic break and stayed at Wood Farm, a remote shooting lodge on the Queen's Sandringham estate in Norfolk. On the Saturday, while Edward was leading a five-hour pheasant shoot, Sophie joined the beaters to pick up the shot birds. More evidence, if it was needed, that Sophie was truly part of 'the Firm' was provided by the Queen herself, when she commented that she found Sophie's company 'Easy, uncomplicated and intelligent.' More importantly, she believed her son's girlfriend was 'good for Ed.'

It's possible that the successful weekend at Wood Farm proved the inspiration for Sophie's first freelance appointment, working on a part-time basis for the Duke of Edinburgh's Award Scheme, of which Prince Edward is chairman, but it's more likely that the plan had been hatched up in advance of her quitting MCM. Naturally, the Palace denied any rumours that she had secured the job, at its offices opposite Windsor Castle, through her connections. Rather, it said quite simply, that she was by far the best candidate for the job.

Beginning immediately, Sophie worked for a few days a week on their quarterly magazine, *Business Award News*, and an 'Outward Bound'

Attending a book launch at Halloween.

newsletter, as well as helping out with the PR side of things. Speaking to the *Daily Mail,* Major-General Michael Hobbs of the Scheme said, 'She's very popular and highly respected. She does a good job and she's paid for it, but she's strictly part-time.' The appointment was the first of many in Sophie's fledgling career. By the end of the year, her portfolio had grown to include accounts for the upmarket catering firm Searcy's and Baby Lifeline, a charity dedicated to providing special baby care and maternity units throughout the country. In addition to this, she also took on some part-time PR consultancy work with the West London marketing firm, Hollander Communications. Sources at the time claimed that her two days a week working for the Duke of Edinburgh Award Scheme brought in around £15,000 per annum, while both Searcy's and Lifeline paid her around £10,000 each. It was a considerable hike in salary for the PR girl.

Rumours

These were exciting times for Sophie. Not only was she in great demand professionally but, three years into their relationship, her daily life was becoming more and more entwined with Edward's. She now divided her time between Buckingham Palace and her flat in West Kensington which, with typical independence, she refused to give up.

Although Sophie had been given her own room in Buckingham Palace, she rarely used it. She preferred to share Edward's bedroom in his second floor apartment (which is visible from the Mall in London, at the top left-hand corner of the building). It's a long way from her Kent home to the grandest Palace in the Kingdom, but Sophie soon took to sharing Edward's apartment – a drawing room, kitchen, bedroom and bathroom – with ease. The two of them would spend hours together there, just cooking, laughing and relaxing comfortably.

The fact that the Royals turned a blind eye to their cohabitation caused some consternation around the country. In April 1996 the Archdeacon of York took it upon himself to denounce the Queen in the Press for setting an immoral example. The Queen refused to enter into debate about the matter,

Sophie often attended the Chelsea Harbour Club to work out.

Sophie, her parents and Prince Edward attend her brother, David's wedding.

and it seems likely that she wanted her youngest son and his girlfriend to enjoy as much privacy as possible in the belief that if and when they did get married, their union would be stronger for it.

The Queen's decision to allow the couple to cohabit at the Palace – something that neither Diana nor Sarah Ferguson were allowed to do – no doubt arose from her steely resolve to let future partners know exactly what they were getting into if they joined the Royal family. Furthermore, the fact that Edward had a girlfriend, and one who was occasionally living with him, helped dispel any speculation that he was gay.

The rumours about Edward's sexuality were persistent, despite the fact that he had had several girlfriends in the past. One of his first, albeit brief, romances had been with a New Zealander called Alison Bell, whom he had met while teaching in her homeland. It had proved a rough first lesson in love when she was caught two-timing him. Naturally enough, there was little contact between them after he left New Zealand. At Cambridge University in the mid-1980s, the prince was often seen with Eleanor Weightman, who gave him the nickname 'Munchkin'. He was next spotted out with the model, Romy Adlington, whom he met in Cowes in 1983.

Three years later, Edward dated Georgia May, daughter of a millionaire boat builder. They too met in Cowes, at the Royal Yacht Squadron Ball. She visited Balmoral and Sandringham, and for a while it was thought that she would be his future bride. After their split, while working at Andrew Lloyd-Webber's Really Useful Theatre Company, Edward met Marsha Bland, a dancer in the musical *Cats*. In 1990, he started dating Ruthie Henshall, then a chorus girl in *Cats*. They went out for a few months, and she issued the standard, we're 'just good friends' statement to the Press. Their friendship lasted quite some time.

Only a few months before meeting Sophie in 1993, Edward was photographed with Astrid Ullens De Schooten Whettnall, the twenty-three-year-old daughter of a Belgian nobleman. The two had met at one of the smartest singles parties ever, a Love Boat cruise round the Norwegian fjords, organized by the King and Queen of Norway.

Despite these well-documented liaisons, the rumour that Edward was gay had been doing the rounds since 1988, when he started working in production for the Really Useful Theatre Company. The fact that he quit the Royal Marines, started working in theatre and was friendly with *Aspects of Love* star, Michael Ball, was enough to keep the story circulating. To add grist to the rumour mill, certain unscrupulous actors claimed that they had slept with Edward. By 1990, Edward had decided enough was enough, and publicly denied the accusations after being interrogated by reporters on a trip to the USA. 'This is so unfair to me and my family,' he said, before adding unequivocally, 'I am not gay.'

His flat-out denial was universally greeted with the response, 'Well, he would say that, wouldn't he?' and, remarkably, denials were still being issued as late as 1996. Friends of the couple were dismayed by the affect the dreadful rumour had upon them singularly and as a couple. Both naturally positive people, having to live with a wave of negativity directed at them with such apparently motiveless malice, was clearly far from easy.

By this time, of course, the Royals were little more than bait for the press sharks circling the Palace. Since the lives of Charles and Di, and Andrew and Fergie had been metaphorically stripped to the bone by the tabloids, the romance of Edward and Sophie must have seemed like fresh meat to them. The Press decided that if Edward wasn't gay, then he could jolly well prove it by announcing his engagement. To this end, the paparazzi started to pursue Sophie relentlessly.

A portrait of her was included in an exhibition entitled 'Leaders of Great Britain into the 21st Century', by photographer Charles Green. Hours before Sophie was due at the preview party at London's ICA gallery, hordes of photographers gathered outside, desperate to take her photograph. Sophie tried to slip in unnoticed, but she was spotted and a cry went up. It was bedlam. Photographers were pushing each other out of the way, desperate to get at her. She stayed for about half an hour, ignoring all the microphones and camera lenses directed at her. 'I would like to stay longer,' she told a friend. 'But the photographers . . . it's unbelievable.'

It made her all the more determined not to attract that kind of personal attention from the media. One friend explained that the couple had, 'Talked for hours about it and [they] know how destructive it can be to try to cultivate a public following. They just want to be themselves.'

Sophie and Tara Palmer Tomkinson at the opening of a new gym.

Speculation was still rife about their relationship, and only became more so when a directive was issued from the Palace stating that they were now co-ordinating her appointments. Anyone who wanted Sophie to attend an event had to direct his or her inquiries to the Prince's private secretary, Lt-Col Sean O'Dwyer.

This was another break in convention, as neither the Princess of Wales nor the Duchess of York had received official support from the Palace until their engagements were announced. And it seemed as if it was not at the Palace's behest, either. 'If you want to invite Sophie to attend something, you should write to Prince Edward's private secretary at the Palace,' said a spokesman. 'Sophie has requested that we put anyone through to that address.' It was a rather smart PR move which gave Sophie more protection from prying eyes and it seemed as if she was really getting the measure of being a Royal consort.

Both Sophie and the Palace were keen to minimize her involvement with the quite relentless paparazzi circus which followed Princess Diana's every move. At that time, the ridiculous question of whether or not Diana had cellulite was taking up acres of newspaper print. Sophie vowed to shape up so that she would never have cause to be mocked for her thighs or waistline. She stopped going to her gym in Chelsea and was soon spotted at the Harbour Club, an exclusive hang out for celebrities and, famously, Princess Diana's former gym.

Sophie had another reason for wanting to look her best, though. Her brother was getting married. In September, David's wedding to Zara Freeland took place in his local church at Northiam, East Sussex, with Edward and Sophie in attendance. David's marriage, though a joyous occasion, must have caused mixed emotions for Sophie. She and her family couldn't have helped wondering if and when she would be following her big brother up the aisle. But Sophie was wise enough to realize that Edward wouldn't be pushed into marriage. The more she pushed, the more he would back off.

Meanwhile, there were other pressures to deal with. During the summer of 1996 the charity that she worked for, Baby Lifeline, was facing ruin, following what proved to be false allegations of financial mismanagement.

The Queen and the Duke of Edinburgh drive the couple to church in Windsor.

The allegations – that in over three years the charity had raised £633,000, but donated only £105,000 to hospitals – had virtually wiped out any more contributions and threatened its very future. It turned out the allegations were due to an accountancy error, and Sophie demonstrated her formidable powers of PR in helping the charity to clear its name. She was thrilled when it was finally given a clean bill of health in September 1996.

Distractions were everywhere for Sophie at this time. Reports had appeared in the papers earlier in the year stating that Prince Edward's father had given him a blunt marriage ultimatum: to make up his mind about Sophie. The Duke of Edinburgh is reported to have said, in his typically forthright manner, 'For God's sake boy, pull your finger out and stop dithering.' The Duke is reported to be very fond of Sophie, telling friends that he thinks she is, 'bloody good fun.' However, even his demands didn't push his son into marriage.

Perhaps Edward didn't feel any need to get married at that time. Why spoil what was clearly a good thing? Hadn't friends (and even family) ruined

The *Spitting Image* programme created puppets of the couple.

perfectly good relationships by marrying? He and Sophie were more relaxed with each other than at any other time in the past three years. As one of Edward's closest friends testified, 'They want to be ordinary, unprecious people, getting on with what they've got. Edward doesn't think it is at all unusual to be in his thirties and not yet married, and Sophie is prepared to wait. She wants to marry him.' One of Sophie's friends remarked, 'The strength of their relationship is that she really does understand Edward, and the fact that while he likes the idea of marriage, he is terrified of it not working.'

Apparently, when asked about his romance a few days after the reports on his father's outburst, Edward was very upset. He told a *Radio Times* interviewer sharply, 'If you shut up, mind your own business and let me do it when I want, it is much more likely to happen. The more people who second-guess, the less likely it is.'

Edward must have begun to think that the whole world was conspiring to marry him off to Sophie. In December, he hosted a party for friends at Wood Farm, and as he looked around the room, it must have occurred to him that of all the couples gathered there, he and Sophie were the only one who were not married. Behind the scenes, though, he was making steps towards greater commitment to the relationship by trying to get to know his girlfriend's family better. He rented a weekend house near Rye in Cinque Port, just twenty miles from Brenchley and quite close to where Sophie's brother, David and his new wife lived.

All the signs were that the couple were in this for the long haul, but that wasn't enough to placate a doggedly inquisitive press. Things were being dragged out far too long for the naturally suspicious newshounds of Fleet Street. Reporting that the couple were spotted at Twickenham watching the Barbarians take on the Australians, questions were asked in print about the true nature of their relationship. Were they really dating? Was this all an elaborate PR stunt dreamed up by Sophie, the resourceful PR expert? The jibes must have hurt the couple enough that they wanted to let everyone know that it was for real: there was no pretence. *Sophie*

Work, Rest & Play

Once again a New Year meant a new beginning for Sophie. She had always been ambitious, and 1997 was the year in which she was to achieve her long-held dream of starting up her own PR company. While freelancing for Hollander Communications, she had met and worked with Murray Harkin, and the two of them developed such a good working relationship that, by 1997, they had decided to go into partnership together under the name of R-JH Public Relations.

Harkin had left Hollander Communications some months earlier and, in January, Sophie decided not to renew her contract with the company. She was free to do whatever she wanted. 'I decided I wanted to set up my own company,' she stated simply. Naturally, questions were asked. Did Sophie want to stop working altogether? Surely an engagement must be imminent? The truth, of course, was that like any other young professional, she wanted to be successful and secure. A freelance career didn't amount to the same thing, no matter how well she did. But owning your own company could offer real proof of success. It was the dream of every middle-class Briton in business: to be your own boss and run things in your own way.

Sophie's business partner, Murray Harkin, outside their Mayfair offices.

Sophie tries to avoid press intrusion as she goes about her work.

For the first six months of 1997, Sophie kept a low public profile as she worked to set up the new company. As with all new ventures, the partners were taking a risk. Sophie hoped that people would take her seriously as a businesswoman and not assume that she would use and abuse her position as Prince Edward's girlfriend. For the owner of a PR company to have such a high profile doesn't always make things easy for clients and can actually work against the company. It was a brave decision but as Sophie later said (*Hello!* magazine, 1997): 'If I joined another company a lot of employees would think I had only got the job because of my personal situation. I decided it was important, as far as my working life was concerned, to be in charge of my own destiny. I like continuity, building relationships where you can see things developing. I love being with people and I get an enormous amount of satisfaction from working with a client and seeing a project through successfully.' Perhaps, as that statement suggests, Sophie felt so powerless in her private life that by setting up her own company and proving her independence, she was showing Edward that she didn't intend to rely on him for the rest of her life and had plenty of other interests.

R-JH PR is located in London's Mayfair and, since its inception, has done extremely well. When launched, the company had only six employees, while today it is a well-established medium-sized agency employing seven consultants and many more staff. The company charges around £10,000 for organizing an event (though it's not known whether they gave the Royal Family a discount for handling the various Royal events they have so far covered). Together, Sophie and Murray have amassed an impressive list of clients, which include The Haven Trust, the breast cancer charity started up by former gallery owner Sara Davenport; the Lanesborough, a landmark London hotel; Thomas Goode, purveyors of silver and glassware, and top jewellers, Boodle and Dunthorpe.

Sophie necessarily had to step up a gear in her working life in order to make the new business a success. That she has made it work is a tribute to her sophisticated PR skills: over the years she has learned how to spot potential problems and avoid them. Knowing the tricks of the trade has also meant that she has further gained the media's respect, not that that's something she'd be foolish enough to brag about: 'I genuinely think the media have been reasonably kind to me,' she has commented, rather hastily adding, 'but then I do lead a normal life.'

However, she had never been able to forestall media questions about the romance between herself and Edward. They had, by now, been an item for over four years. Many Royal watchers were predicting that, on their return from a summer break to St Tropez that year, Sophie would at last be wearing a ring on her finger. However, these predictions were to be proved wrong yet again.

Speculation about the relationship was constantly being fuelled by statements from the Palace, both official and unofficial. 'Even the Royal Household say she is good news and that is praise indeed,' said one such unofficial 'spokesman'. 'Sophie will not disturb the status quo of the monarchy and that is what is important.'

Not disturbing the status quo had been the primary concern of the Windsors ever since details of the breakdown of Charles and Diana's marriage had started to become public several years before. But they were losing the battle. Diana, it was generally thought, had outmanoeuvred the Royals in the battle to win the hearts and minds of the British people, and now she was making bigger headlines than ever before. Photographs of the former Princess of Wales lounging in the sun with playboy, Dodi Al Fayed, son of Harrod's owner, Mohammed Al Fayed, had been appearing in newspapers across the world for the past couple of weeks. The good news for Edward and Sophie was that at least Diana's new romance diverted any press attention away from them. Speculation as to whether Diana and Dodi's relationship would eventually lead to marriage was now reaching a worldwide frenzy. However, tragedy was about to strike.

In the early hours of Sunday morning, 31 August 1997, Princess Diana and Dodi were killed in a car crash in Paris. The whole nation – indeed the world – was in shock over the terrible accident and the senseless waste of life. For the next year Britain mourned its 'Queen of Hearts' and it was inconceivable that Edward and Sophie should even consider making a wedding announcement during that time.

Prior to the fatal accident, Sophie had often been compared to Diana by the Press and even her friends had commented on a certain resemblance.

Sophie on a PR commission in Fulham, West London.

Sophie attends a party at the Natural History Museum in 1999.

Addressing the subject in *Hello!* magazine, she had said: 'Well, she's [Diana] described as one of the world's most beautiful women, so I can only take it as a flattering comment. But I don't try to emulate the way she looks or dresses. I've been likened to her from the first day she stepped into the public eye, therefore it was absolutely no surprise when the media picked up on it.' Sophie's passing resemblance had, of course, been played up by an hysterical press, one tabloid famously describing her as being 'Di-dentical' from the moment she appeared at Edward's side.

In fact, there are more differences than similarities between the two. At only 5ft 5in, Sophie is somewhat shorter and more pear-shaped than Diana, who stood an elegant 5ft 10in in her stockinged feet. Furthermore, Sophie is fifteen years older than Diana was when she became engaged to Prince Charles, and is vastly more experienced in both handling the media and mixing with the Royals. Finally, of course, Sophie is marrying a younger son and so does not have to face the pressure of becoming the future queen.

When all the hysteria surrounding Diana's death eventually subsided, newspapers – finding themselves now short of dramatic Royal coverage – resumed their commentary on Edward's lack of commitment to Sophie. Once again friends of the couple were forced into making polite statements about the relationship. One such friend said, 'Marriage is the most likely conclusion, but at the moment nothing is set in stone so Sophie has to make the most of her opportunities.' Another one of Edward's friends confirmed for about the umpteenth time that, 'He wants Sophie and himself to be a successful professional couple, living their own lives in their own way – just like his cousins, Lady Sarah Chatto and her husband, Dan, and Lady Helen Taylor with Tim.'

And so yet another year had passed without an announcement of an impending Royal wedding.

Bless This House

Sophie was now a successful businesswoman and Edward, too, could point to the continuing success of his TV production company. Another of the possible prerequisites of marriage had been met. As if to celebrate this, Edward set out to buy a family home, where both he and Sophie could settle down together and from where he could also run his business, Ardent Productions.

Edward took on a £50,000-a-year lease on Bagshot Park, a Crown Estate property. He was attracted by the privacy of the place – it stands in eighty-seven acres of parkland and adjoins farmland and forestry with south-facing views of Sandhurst and Camberley – and the pastoral scenes which would remind Sophie of her own home, back in Kent. Edward also gained planning permission to convert the stable block into an office space.

In 1877, Benjamin Ferry designed the Victorian mock Tudor house for Arthur, Duke of Connaught, Queen Victoria's youngest son. After the Duke's death in 1942, none of the Royals wanted the house, and it became part of the Royal Army Chaplains Department. Edward would return Bagshot to the Royal housing stock when he left.

Prince Edward shown outside Bagshot Park, the couple's new home.

Only eleven miles from Windsor and within easy commuting distance to London, Edward decided that Bagshot had everything that the couple could possibly require in their first home. 'The sense of solace is terrific,' Edward enthused. 'And I like the fact that the house will give me the chance to bring back a former Royal residence.' Edward made it clear that his plans for the house involved reinstating the character of a residence built for a Royal duke: 'It will require imagination and that little bit of extra effort. There is no point in just diving in and giving it an extra coat of paint.'

In August 1998, the couple hired their friend, Mary Montagu, the only daugher of Lord Montagu of Beaulieu, as the interior designer of their new home. Edward and Mary worked closely together on the designs for the

Sophie remains unpretentious in the glare of the public spotlight.

house, while Sophie also took a hands-on approach, starting to put forward ideas for the colour schemes and furnishings. Mary spent a lot of time with the couple, trying to get an idea of Sophie's and Edward's likes and dislikes in order to create a new home just to their liking. 'This should be a family home for the year 2000,' said Mary. 'It won't be an over-the-top English country house, [but] more classical with a modern twist.'

As with everything that the couple did, the cost of the project aroused a great deal of interest. But Edward defended his reluctance to discuss the financial aspects of his proposals on the grounds of privacy. 'If it was going to involve public money,' he said, 'people ought to know. But since it won't, but is a private venture, that is how it should stand.'

Naturally, all this activity at Bagshot Park stirred up yet more speculation about a possible engagement. The couple had now been together for five years and everyone was holding their breath for the announcement. There seemed to be no more royal upsets on the horizon and Edward's siblings had all found happiness with new (or in Charles's case, old) partners. The furore surrounding Diana's death had finally subsided, and it had even been publicly accepted that Charles was now seeing Camilla Parker-Bowles. It appeared there were no further impediments to the marriage remaining, so why was Edward still prevaricating?

A so-called 'friend' of Sophie's suggested that the delay was beginning to affect even her. 'Sophie is upset about it, naturally,' said the source, who added that, 'Sophie and all of us really thought it would be happening this year, but Edward has said quite firmly that marriage will have to wait.'

Speaking from his new offices at Bagshot, Edward trenchantly made his position clear: 'I have enough on my plate. They [an engagement and a new family home] are totally separate issues. Obviously, if that changes, no doubt I shall have to tell people. But however much tempted, please do not read too much into this in terms of any changes in my private life, certainly not at this stage. This is not some sort of circuitous route of changing my private life. These things will be announced when the time comes, not before.'

Sophie continued about her business as normally as she was able to do. However, her position as a Royal-in-waiting was beginning to have a knock-on effect on her work. Since Edward's forthright statement to the media did nothing to quell any engagement rumours, the paparazzi were still hot on Sophie's trail. One celebrity who witnessed Sophie's media standing at close quarters was the former lottery presenter, Anthea Turner. In July, Anthea was supposed to be the centre of attention at the promotional launch of a breast cancer charity. However, she found herself somewhat upstaged by the PR officer who had arranged the photocall – Sophie Rhys-Jones.

Dozens of photographers converged on the Fulham church for the photocall, yet when Anthea turned up (the *London Evening Standard*), photographers put down their cameras, making it clear that they were not there for her at all. Sophie tried to escape from all the attention by quickly disappearing into the church. Naturally, she must have been incredibly disappointed by all this. She just wanted to get on with her job and could only apologize profusely to Anthea and to the charity involved.

Despite the resurgence of media interest in herself and Edward, Sophie attempted to carry on as normally as she could. At the launch of the China Jazz restaurant in Berkeley Square, where builders hadn't finished their work, guests arrived to find her dusting and tidying up wearing a black beaded top and slim-line trousers from Tomasz Starzewski's collection. It was just as if she was with her old friends in Stoke Fleming and they needed a hand. As all her friends testify, Sophie had hardly changed during her years in the public spotlight. She remained hard-working and unpretentious, and had always got on with the job at hand. For that alone, she earned the respect of her colleagues.

As the fifth year of their courtship came to an end, there was at last an engagement announcement in sight. *Sophie*

Tania Bryer, Sophie and Catrina Skepper at a launch party.

The Dream Realized

The 6th of January 1999 proved to be a beautiful morning. As the sun shone, taking the bite out of a crisp, wintry air, Sophie and Edward walked gracefully towards the cameras lined up before them in the grounds of St James's Gardens in London. They were there to display a magnificent diamond engagement ring.

News of the engagement had already been leaked by the *Sun* newspaper that morning, pre-empting the 10 a.m. confirmation from Buckingham Palace. The statement read: 'The Queen and The Duke of Edinburgh are delighted to announce the engagement of their youngest son, Prince Edward, to Miss Sophie Rhys-Jones. The couple sought the permission of their respective parents between Christmas and the New Year. Both families are thrilled at the news. No decision has been taken yet regarding the venue and date for the wedding. However, Prince Edward and Miss Rhys-Jones hope that it might be possible to use St George's Chapel, Windsor, in the late spring or summer.'

Which only left the photocall. The bright, spring-like weather that day complemented the couple's apparent joy at the announcement. A thousand

Hand-in-hand, the happy couple step out for the engagement photocall.

camera flashes reflected off both the small encrusted stones on Sophie's slate-grey Tomasz Starzewski suit and the diamonds in her engagement ring. An eighteen-carat white-gold ring with a large oval diamond, flanked by two smaller, heart-shaped diamonds, it came from the Royal jewellers, Asprey & Garrard, and cost Edward £55,000.

Edward's happy mood was obvious as he quipped to the gathered crowd, 'Diamonds are a girl's best friend, so I'm told.' Sophie, bubbling with laughter, immediately riposted, 'No, you're my best friend.'

Throughout the press conference Edward kept a tight hold of Sophie's hand as they laughed and smiled at each other. Again, they were asked: 'Why do you get on so well together?' Edward replied, 'I don't know, we just do, really,' but Sophie added, 'I think we share a lot of interests, we laugh a lot, we have a good friendship.'

Another reporter asked him why it had taken him so long to propose. 'It's impossible for anyone else to understand why it has taken me this long,' answered Edward. 'But, I don't think Sophie would have said yes if I had asked before, and hopefully by the fact that she did say yes, I must have got the timing right.'

One reporter suggested that he didn't want to lose his bachelor status and had been enjoying his freedom. Edward laughed loudly and, putting his arm around Sophie, replied, 'If I'm not ready for it now, it's too late. We are the very best of friends and that's essential, and it also helps that we happen to love each other as well, very much. We're very happy at the moment, and long may that continue.'

They were then questioned about the pressures they would have to face, considering the breakdown of all Edward's siblings' marriages. 'Oh, somebody had to bring that up, didn't they?' he said, turning to Sophie, with another laugh. 'More pressure? I don't know. If anybody's going to get married, I hope that they think that they are going to get it right.'

If Edward sounded a little unsure, that may be a sign of maturity rather than a reluctance to commit. In fact, he had made up his mind to propose to Sophie only a matter of weeks beforehand. Just before Christmas, and without Sophie's knowledge, he had travelled to see her parents in Brenchley and had asked for their daughter's hand in marriage. Naturally, this was just a formality, albeit an important one for both parties. Her parents agreed to keep the engagement a secret so that Sophie wouldn't know about Edward's visit. When the news broke, Christopher told the Press, 'We are both extremely pleased and very happy for Sophie and Prince Edward. We have always enjoyed Prince Edward's company and feel that they make a wonderful couple.'

That the Rhys-Jones's kept Edward's secret was recalled with glee by the Prince: 'She had no idea that it was coming, which was what I really wanted,' he smiled. 'I mean, the trouble is, everybody always speculating, which has always made it very difficult. Every time there was another round of speculation, I had to go very quiet again.' Re-living the moment when Edward proposed, Sophie told those gathered, 'I was slightly stunned for a minute. Then I suddenly realized that I should answer the question. I said "Yes, yes, please." '

There were still those who assumed – incorrectly, of course – that the only reason that Sophie and Edward were now engaged was due to the fact that she had issued him with an ultimatum: marry me or else. During the photocall, Sophie was adamant that this hadn't been the case and tried to set the record straight: 'Contrary to popular opinion we've never lived together and I've never issued any ultimatums,' she said with a smile. (In 1995 Sophie confessed to her old friend, Eon Balmain that she had no intention of cracking under the pressure. She told the Aussie designer, Eon: 'I am not going through all this for nothing.' Source: the *Sun*.)

There was yet more laughter when Edward was asked about starting his own family. 'Let's take one step at a time,' he said, and continued laughing while Sophie, with a little twinkle in her eye, reminded the Press that, 'We're not married yet.' As if it needed asking, the question of how Sophie felt about becoming a Windsor was raised. 'It is slightly nerve-racking in many ways,' she replied. 'But I am ready for it now and I am fully aware of the responsibilities and commitments.'

Which only left the matter of where the wedding was to be held. Would Sophie's father be hiring Westminster Abbey? Or perhaps the Royal Family would be happy to attend the wedding ceremony in her local church, All Saints in Brenchley? The latter was a possibility given that Edward would

Sophie and Edward are evidently overjoyed by their engagement.

prefer a 'quiet' family wedding. After much pressing he finally revealed where he would like the wedding to be held: 'I expect I'm going to be deeply unpopular,' he began. 'I have always enjoyed St George's and Windsor especially. It's a wonderful setting, a glorious piece of architecture and is somewhere slightly different.' Sophie's response to the matter of location was somewhat less specific: 'I think getting married is a very personal thing. Naturally, there is going to be more interest in us than with other people, but it is a family occasion.'

Windsor is certainly an important place for the couple, where they have been able to spend quiet, romantic weekends together. But there was always pressure for them to have a very public Royal wedding involving the whole nation, an event that would invoke memories of previous Royal weddings. That, of course, may be just what Edward didn't want, given the eventual outcome of the marriages of Charles, Anne and Andrew.

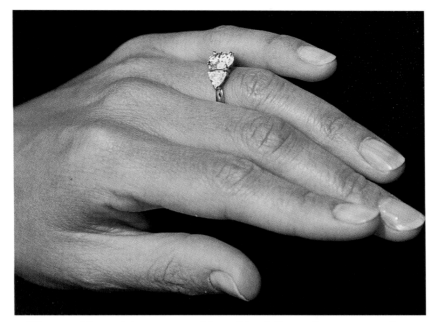

The magnificent eighteen-carat white-gold and diamond engagement ring.

As the press conference ended, the happy couple walked back to the Palace. Still hand-in-hand, they created a quite memorable image of almost Hollywood proportions: that of a man and woman walking happily together into the future.

Soon after the announcement, Sophie moved into Buckingham Palace and this time she was given her own suite of rooms, near to the Prince's apartment on the second floor. It happened so quickly that she just had to ring a close friend to say, 'One minute I was in rubber gloves cleaning my flat, the next I'm moving into my new place.' When the friend asked her where, she said, 'Where do you think? – the Palace, of course!'

Sophie

Business As Usual

As soon as the engagement was announced, well-wishers passed on their congratulations. One former colleague of Prince Edward, from the Really Useful Theatre Company days, told the *Sun*, 'Edward always dreamed of being an ordinary bloke. That's all he ever really wanted. He insisted on being referred to as plain "Edward Windsor", but he was always very much aware of the gulf his family background created. Sophie's down-to-earth attitude was just what he was looking for.'

The Prime Minister, Tony Blair, issued a short, diplomatic statement which simply said, 'They are a delightful couple and I am sure they will be very happy together.' One of Sophie's old school friends commented that, 'Knowing her from our school days, I am convinced that she is marrying for love, not because of any Royal connections. She's not that kind of girl.'

It looked like being a busy year for Edward. His career and his company, Ardent Productions, were now in full swing and he had just completed renovating Bagshot Park to house his office. After six years in business, Ardent Productions, which specializes in historical documentaries, was in profit for the very first time.

Sophie arrives for work on her 34th birthday.

Likewise, things looked just as hectic for Sophie, who showed no signs of wanting to give up her job. Indeed, her business partner, Murray Harkin said, 'She works very hard and all hours. Even if she has children I think she'll carry on working. Sophie is very mature and watches everything she does and says, which is why she will make a particularly good bride for Edward. I've never seen her so happy.'

Five days after the engagement announcement, Sophie slipped out of a large Rover car for a short walk to work in London's Mayfair. Showing all the poise of a professional Royal, she joked with the reporters and the multitude of photographers, who were surrounding her and blocking her path. Well-wishers clutching bouquets struggled with police and journalists as they tried to get closer to the Royal-bride-to-be.

The couple still hadn't confirmed the date for the ceremony and as the camera flashes went off in her face, temporarily blinding her, Sophie informed the crowd, 'You'll know when we set a date.' Then, with an air of calm, she turned to one of the reporters, who had asked if, 'All this media focus on her is to be expected, isn't it?' She smiled and replied, 'I am thinking of contacting Insomniacs International.'

Struggling towards the R-JH office in South Audley Street, Sophie explained why she wanted to keep on working: 'I have set this company up and I have commitments to clients and staff, and I want to carry that on.' Replying to the question of what it would be like to be part of a Royal marriage, she said, 'I will see about that when it happens.'

Finally, she reached the door of her office, only to find that it wouldn't open. No matter how hard she tried, nothing worked. Admitting defeat, she had to plead, 'Will somebody let me in,' through the intercom.

The Press were continually asking questions of the couple in the weeks following the engagement. Of course, the question had changed. Now it wasn't so much, 'When are you getting married, Sophie?' but, 'What will you wear?' Ever the professional, she would invariably smile and reply, 'I don't normally give out those kind of details. I prefer to keep them private,' and disappear into yet another PR event.

As ever, the couple wanted to celebrate the engagement as privately as possible, but both knew what they were letting themselves in for. In fact, when Sophie was asked if she was looking forward to the high-profile attention she was going to receive during her marriage to Edward, she replied boldly, 'Yes, I am.' (Said the *Daily Mail*, on Sophie's choice, prior to the announcement: 'She has one objective in life and that is to marry Prince Edward. Every decision she makes in her personal and her professional life is geared towards that. It makes her extremely cautious about her image. But she knows how to manage it so that she comes across as the person the Royal Family wants her to be. She has been accused of becoming grand, but let's face it, if you were an ordinary middle-class girl from Kent and you found yourself mixing with Her Majesty and Lord this and Princess that, then you would have to adapt your behaviour.')

Apparently Sophie asked the Queen if it was possible, after the wedding, not to be referred to as the Princess Edward. Instead, many royal experts predict that the Queen will make Edward a duke, in turn bestowing upon Sophie the title of duchess.

Whatever her official title, carrying on at work is going to be a real test for her. As a Royal 'insider' pointed out, 'Her business path will be littered with potentially damaging conflicts of interest. At this stage no one wants to be a killjoy and it's not just about being old-fashioned.'

It could be argued that for the last five years, Sophie's Royal contacts had made her services attractive to companies eager to capitalize on her standing. But it's equally true that she had been impressing clients as a consummate PR for a long time before she became a Royal girlfriend.

Often perhaps, it was a combination of both her contacts and her skills which made her such a success in her field. She won her Thomas Goode contract – the company sells upmarket porcelain and chinaware from its Mayfair shop – after meeting managing director, Rumi Verjee, who was impressed enough to ask her to organize events for him. A source close to Rumi told the *Daily Mail*, 'The company wanted to see its wares promoted to a younger generation and it was felt that Sophie, with her PR skills and Royal connections, would be ideal. Her friends are just the sort of people they are targeting.'

The worry was that when Sophie became a Royal herself she would be invited to take on new accounts for companies and individuals who might want her to organize events or take part in public activities which could be seen as potentially embarrassing to the Royal Family. People who knew Sophie, however, could have no such worries. She was smart enough to know when a job was not worth taking. After all, she hadn't made any slip-ups in the past five years.

Meanwhile on 17 January, Sophie and Edward were seen walking down the aisle together. In their first public appearance since the announcement, the happy couple were attending Sandringham parish church with various members of the Royal family. A crowd of about fifty well-wishers called out congratulations to the pair as they entered the church, where Sophie joined the front rank of the Royal Family for the first time. She had even led the way to the church in line with Prince Philip and Prince Edward.

Not long after this, it was business as usual for the couple. Among a string of other PR parties and launches which she attended, Sophie organized an exclusive 250th birthday party for the wine merchants, Justerini and Brooks. The party was held at the Natural History Museum, where Sophie told the *London Evening Standard*, 'Engaged life is rather nice. I recommend it.'

She was quite happy to chat about the changes in her life since the engagement, revealing that, 'The biggest difference [in my life] is the amount of correspondence I've received. So many people have written to say congratulations, so I'm spending my whole time writing thank-you notes.' She went on, 'I can't think too far ahead to the wedding yet, but I'm looking forward to joining the Royal Family. They're all so nice.'

It is quite possible that, of all the Royal unions of the recent past, this one looks best set from the start. Sophie has a lot in her favour. Unlike Princess Diana and Sarah Ferguson, she is a mature thirtysomething bride, who has spent a lot of time with the Royal Family and now knows them all well. She shares their interests, their desire for privacy and also their respect for convention. As the Prince's biographer, Ingrid Seward, said, 'Edward and Sophie have been together for such a long time. They will have discovered anything they didn't like about each other and couldn't live with.'

Sophie attends the Queen's Anniversary Lunch with Prince William.

Happy Endings...

There has been a castle at Windsor for over 900 years. After the Norman Conquest, the new King William chose the site, high above the River Thames on the edge of a Saxon hunting ground, because of its proximity to London. It is only a hard day's march, and a shorter boat trip away, from the capital, whose west flank it was originally built to guard.

Naturally, the historic building is reputed to have its share of Royal ghosts, including King Henry VIII, Queen Elizabeth I, King Charles I and King George III (mad King George). It has a grand Royal history, which is partly why Edward so wanted Sophie to walk down the aisle of St George's Chapel on 19 June 1999.

St George's Chapel lies within the castle walls and is a revered Royal shrine, and the resting-place of ten sovereigns of the Crown. Founded by Edward IV in 1475 and completed in 1528 by Henry VIII, the Chapel is dedicated to the patron saint of the Order of the Garter, Britain's highest Order of Chivalry, and contains knights' banners, stall plates, magnificent woodwork and stone vaulting. Some say that the Chapel ranks among the

St George's Chapel, Windsor Castle, the venue for the couple's wedding.

Sophie attends an official ceremony looking every inch a Royal.

finest examples of Perpendicular Gothic, the late mediaeval style of English architecture.

The Chapel itself is stunning. There are huge, stained-glass windows that light up the whole of the nave (on the wedding day Sophie will be serenaded by the choir, with candles lighting the way). The St George's Chapel Choir has existed at Windsor for over 600 years. Choristers all attend St George's School, which is also within the precincts of the Castle. The twelve lay-clerks of the choir (four altos, four tenors and four basses) reside in the Horseshoe Cloister, a group of timbered houses built round a courtyard, in the shape of the horseshoe badge of King Edward IV.

The Chapel hosts the annual Service of the Order of the Garter, when the Knights of the Order, together with HM The Queen, make a procession through the Castle to the Chapel for their Festival Service.

It was here, in 1992, that Edward so enjoyed the wedding of Lady Helen Windsor to Tim Taylor and, in 1997, Prince William's confirmation took place. The Prince's confirmation brought about the first official photograph since 1993 in which his parents, Charles and Diana and the Queen were pictured together.

It is a truly stunning location for a wedding. Windsor is a fairy tale of a castle, set in the rolling green hills of Berkshire, with large towers that rise up over the Thames. As Sophie and her father arrive for the ceremony after their drive through the King Henry VIII Gate, these towers will dominate the setting for the wedding.

When Sophie reaches the chapel and prepares to walk through the nave from the Great West Door, she will see the choir and opposite them, the senior members of the Royal Family in order of precedence, with the Queen and the Duke of Edinburgh nearest their future daughter-in-law. Waiting for Sophie in the centre near the High Altar will, of course, be her future husband, Prince Edward Anthony Richard Louis Windsor – or, as he prefers to be known, Edward Windsor.

If their wedding goes ahead as originally planned, Edward will be the first of the Queen's sons to marry in private. Charles and Diana's wedding was watched by 500 million TV viewers, while his brother, Andrew and Sarah Ferguson's union attracted 20 million. Edward is particularly keen to ban cameras from the Chapel, feeling that if he allows them in, he is inviting the media into his marriage – and neither he nor Sophie wants to give anyone that kind of access.

Edward is so anxious to restrict the TV cameras that he wants to limit them to covering the arrival and departure of their 500 guests. Both he and Sophie want the occasion to be a family affair, not a pompous Royal procession. And if they succeed in banning the world's TV, then the young couple would be setting a precedent which shows the next generation of Windsors how they could live their lives – freely, with little interference from the rest of the world.

If Edward's well-laid plans work accordingly, then the marriage of the youngest son of the ruling family of Great Britain to a smart, sassy, fun-loving girl from Brenchley would represent something truly wonderful. In so far as he can, he would finally fulfil his dream – of being a normal person and living an ordinary life.

For Sophie Rhys-Jones, 19 June 1999 will be the fulfilment of another dream altogether. The small child who dreamed of ponies, princes and being loved by everybody will have found that happy endings do exist.

Let us hope that her fairy tale ends with a happy ever after...

After the press conference, the couple walk happily into the future together.

Picture Credits

The author and publishers have made every reasonable effort to contact all copyright holders.
Any errors that may have occurred are inadvertent and anyone who for any reason has not
been contacted is invited to write to the publishers so that a full acknowledgement may be
made in subsequent editions of this work.